LETTERS OF INTENT

INTRODUCTION

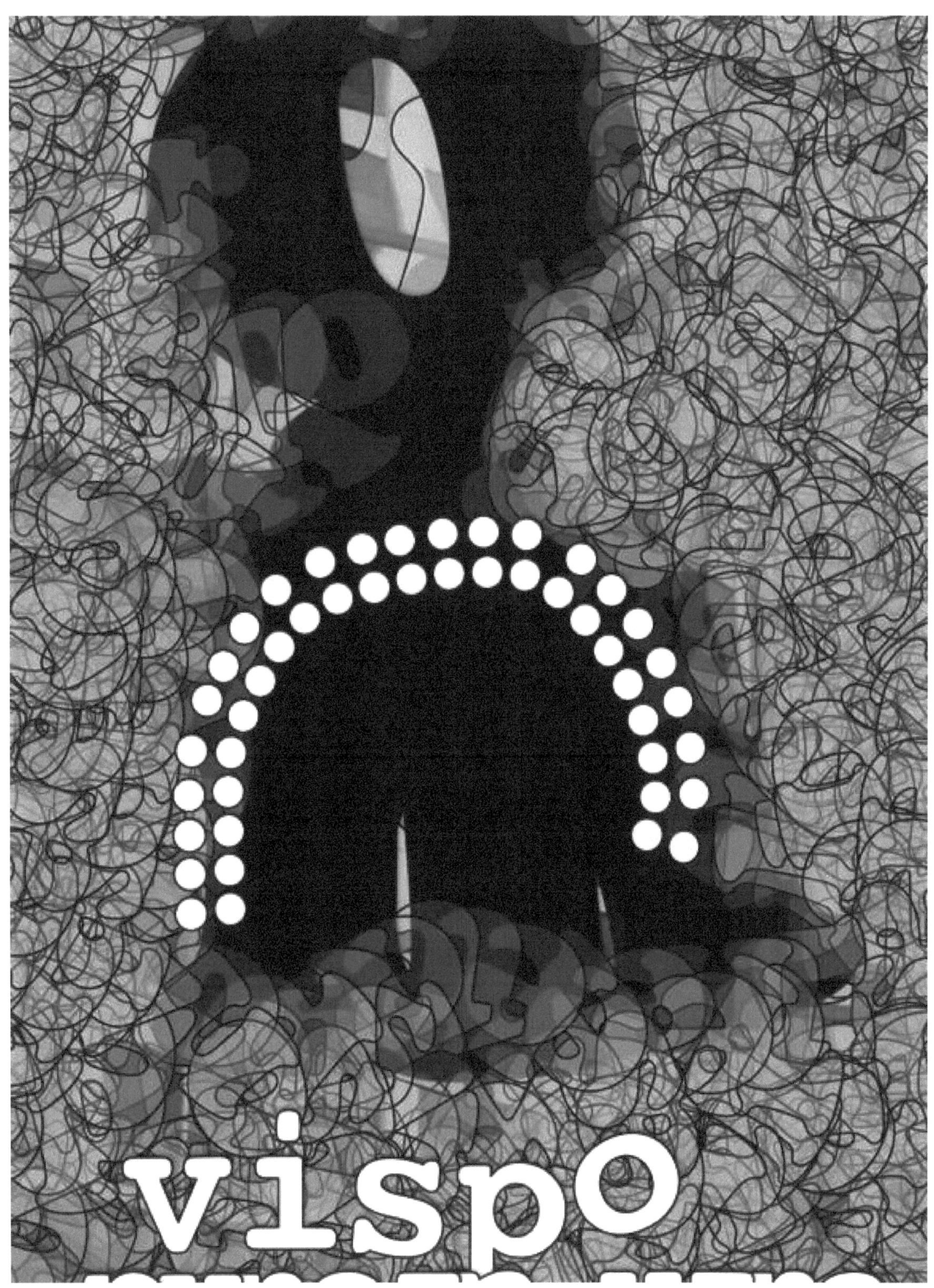
vispo

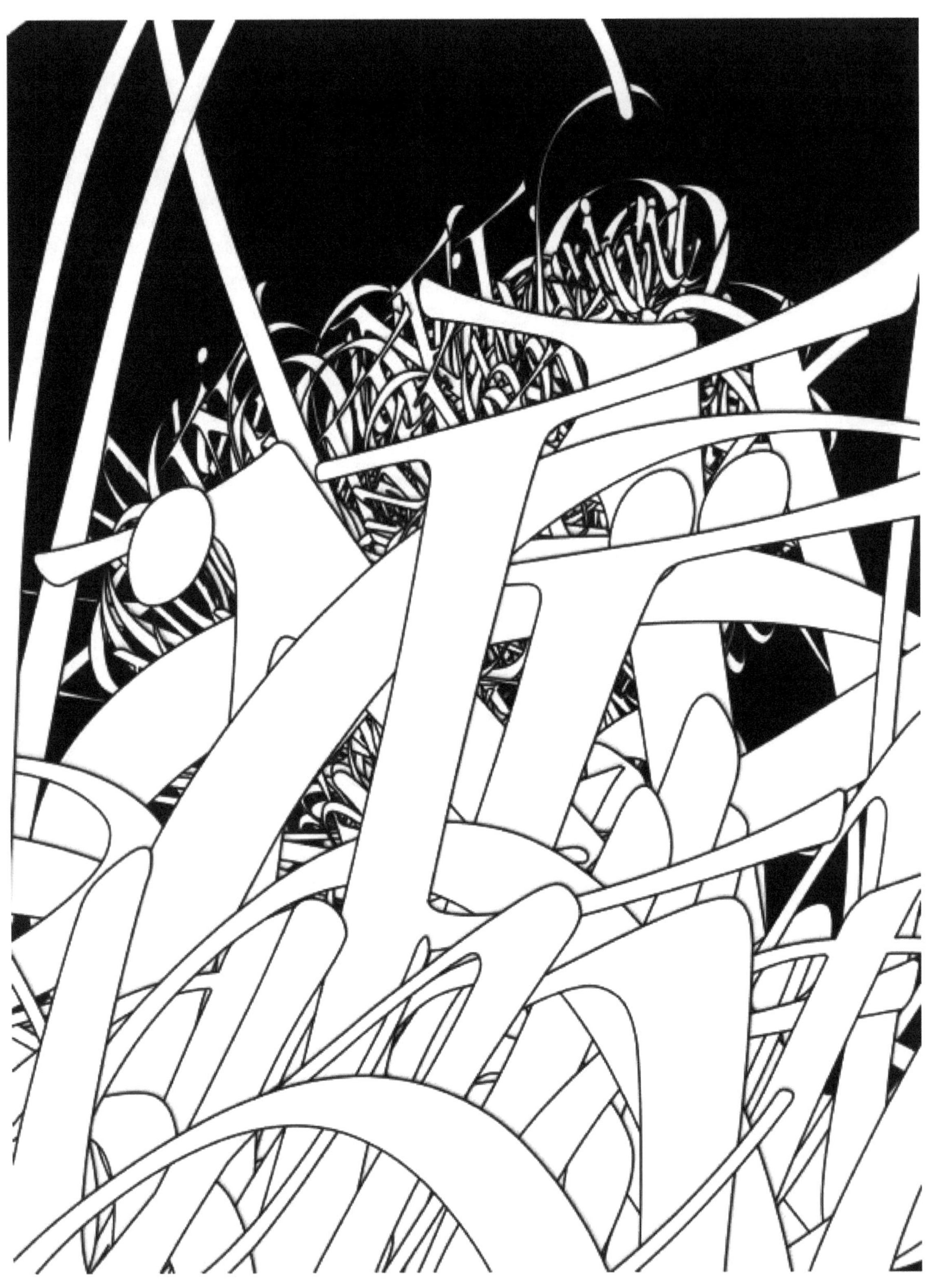

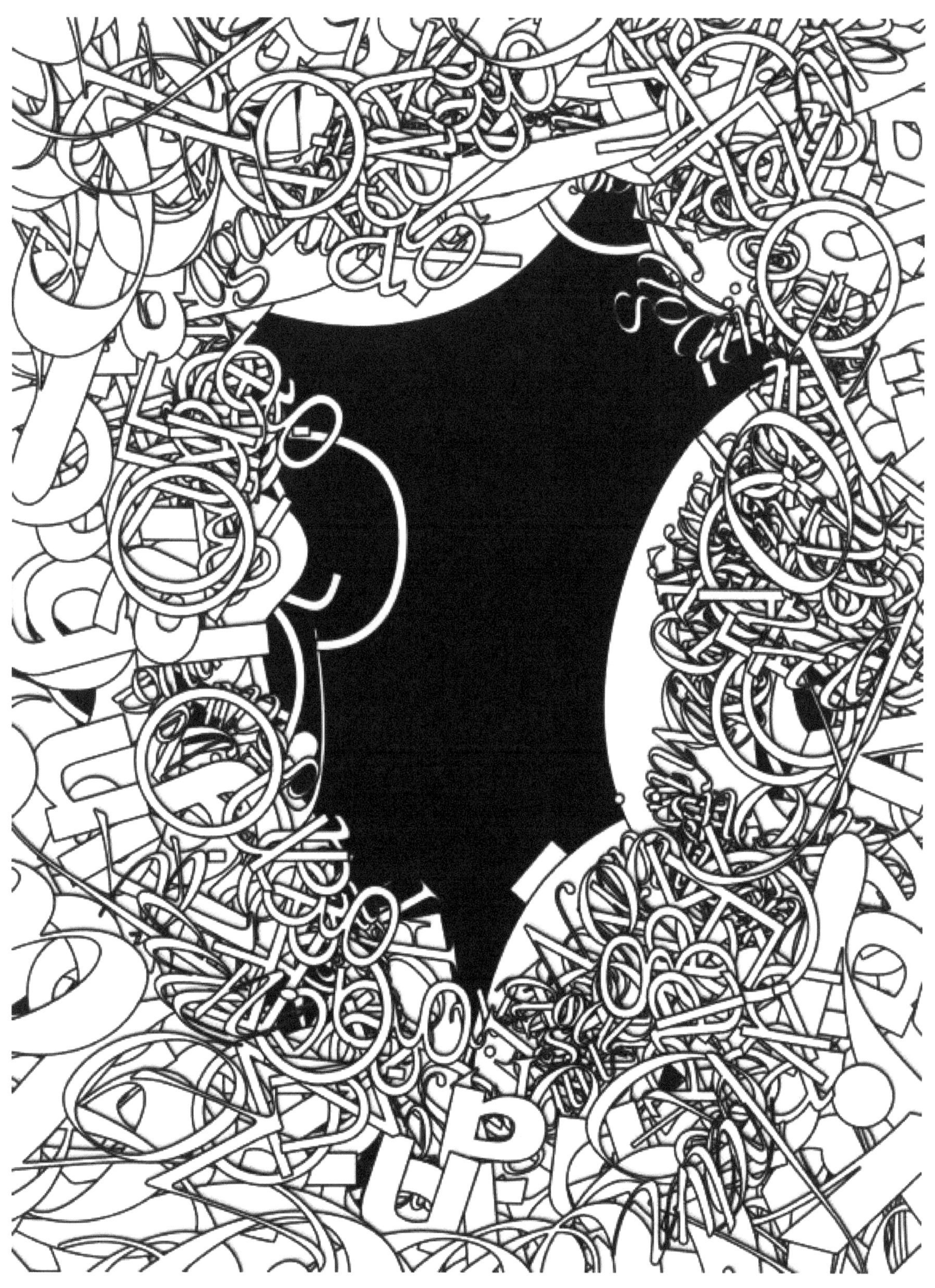

COINS

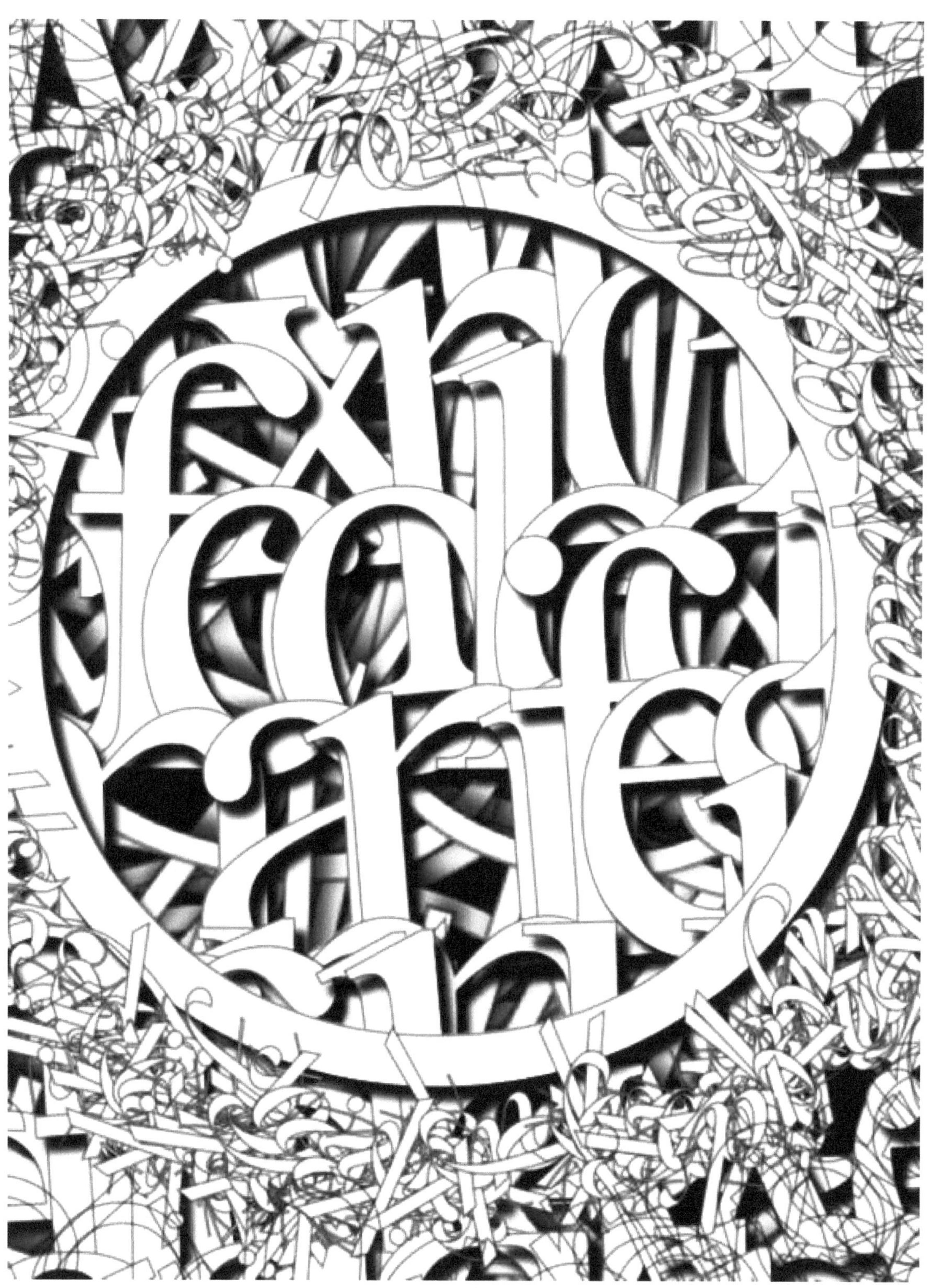

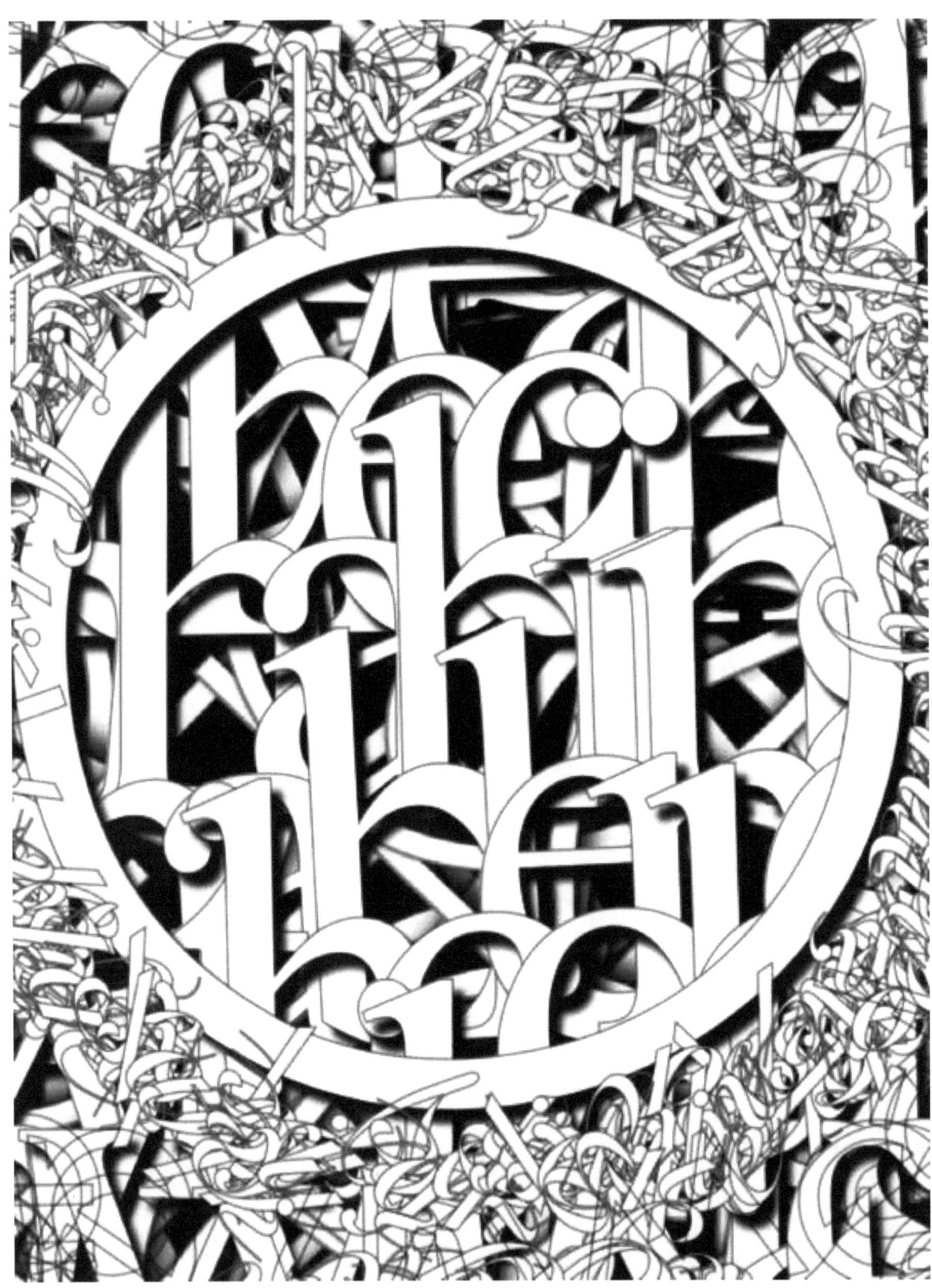

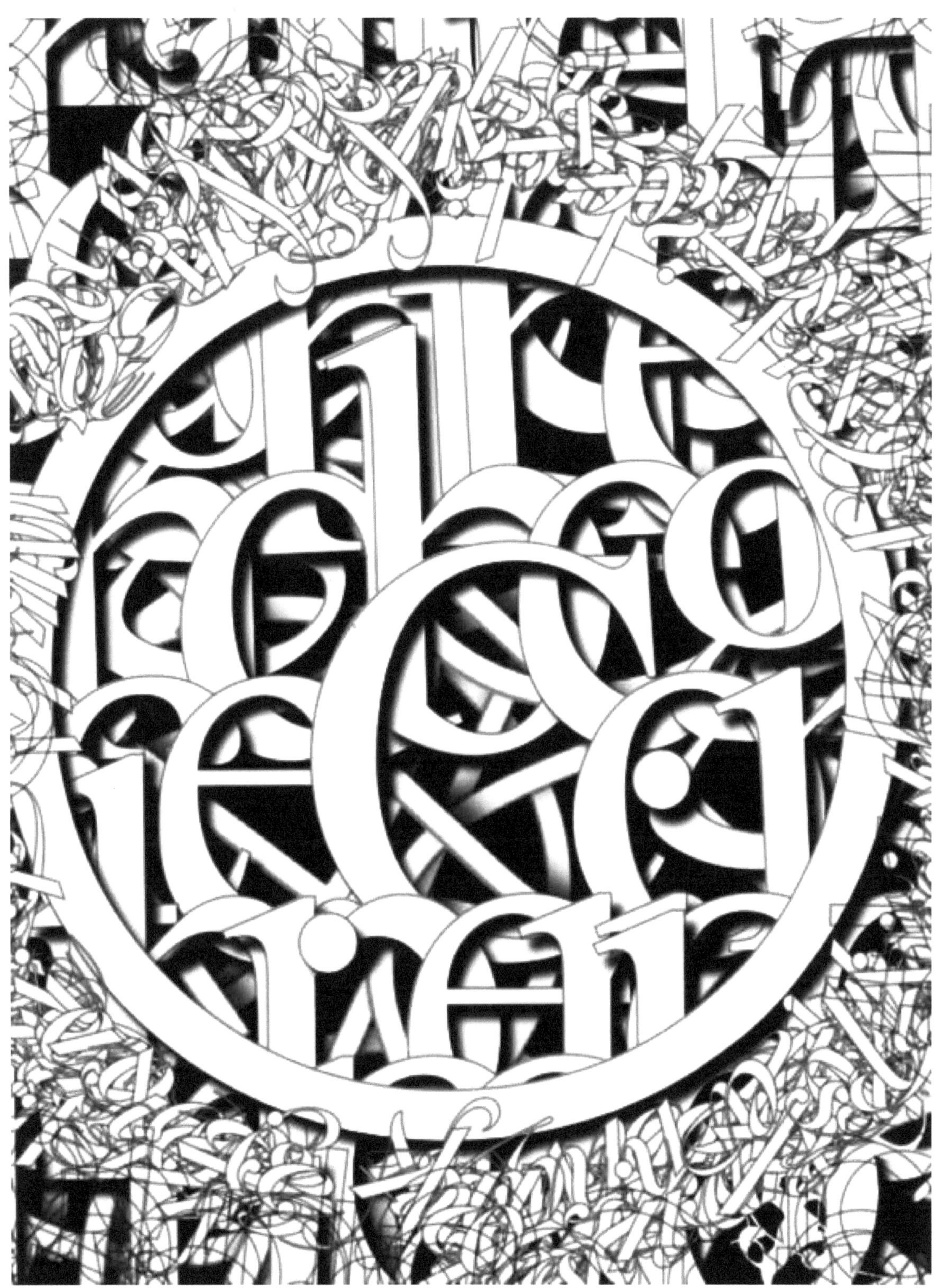

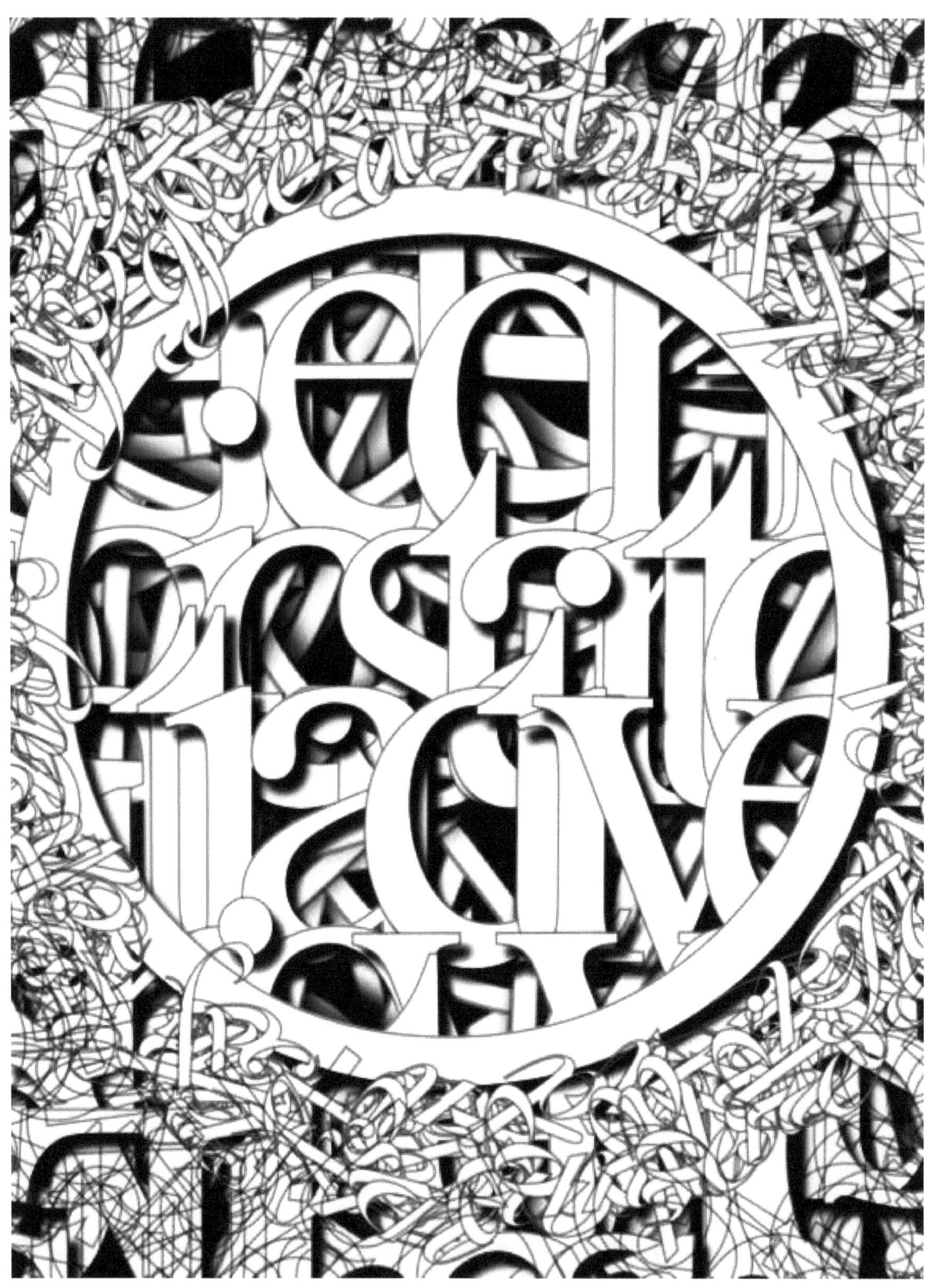

DETERIORATA/ACCUMULATA

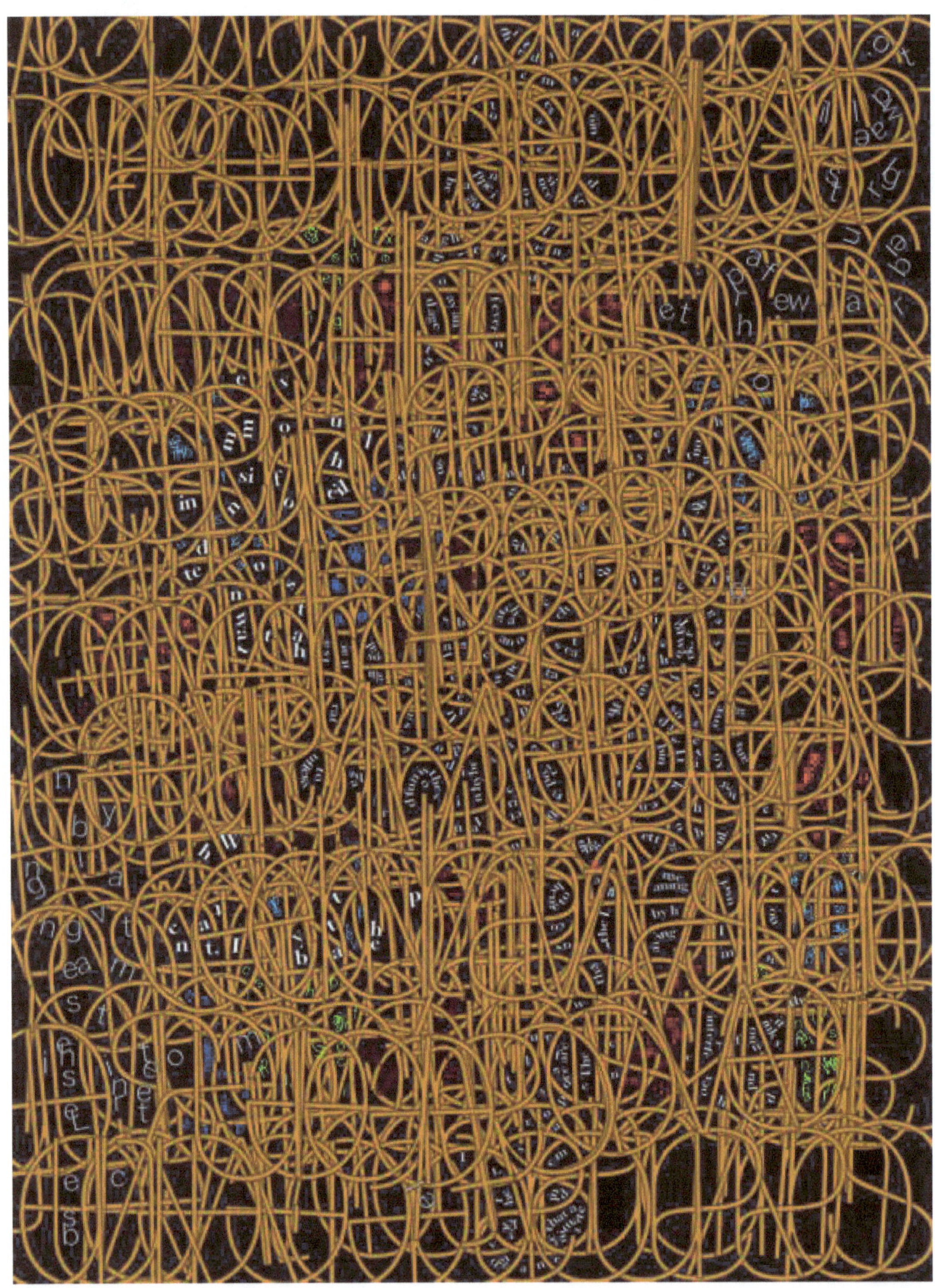

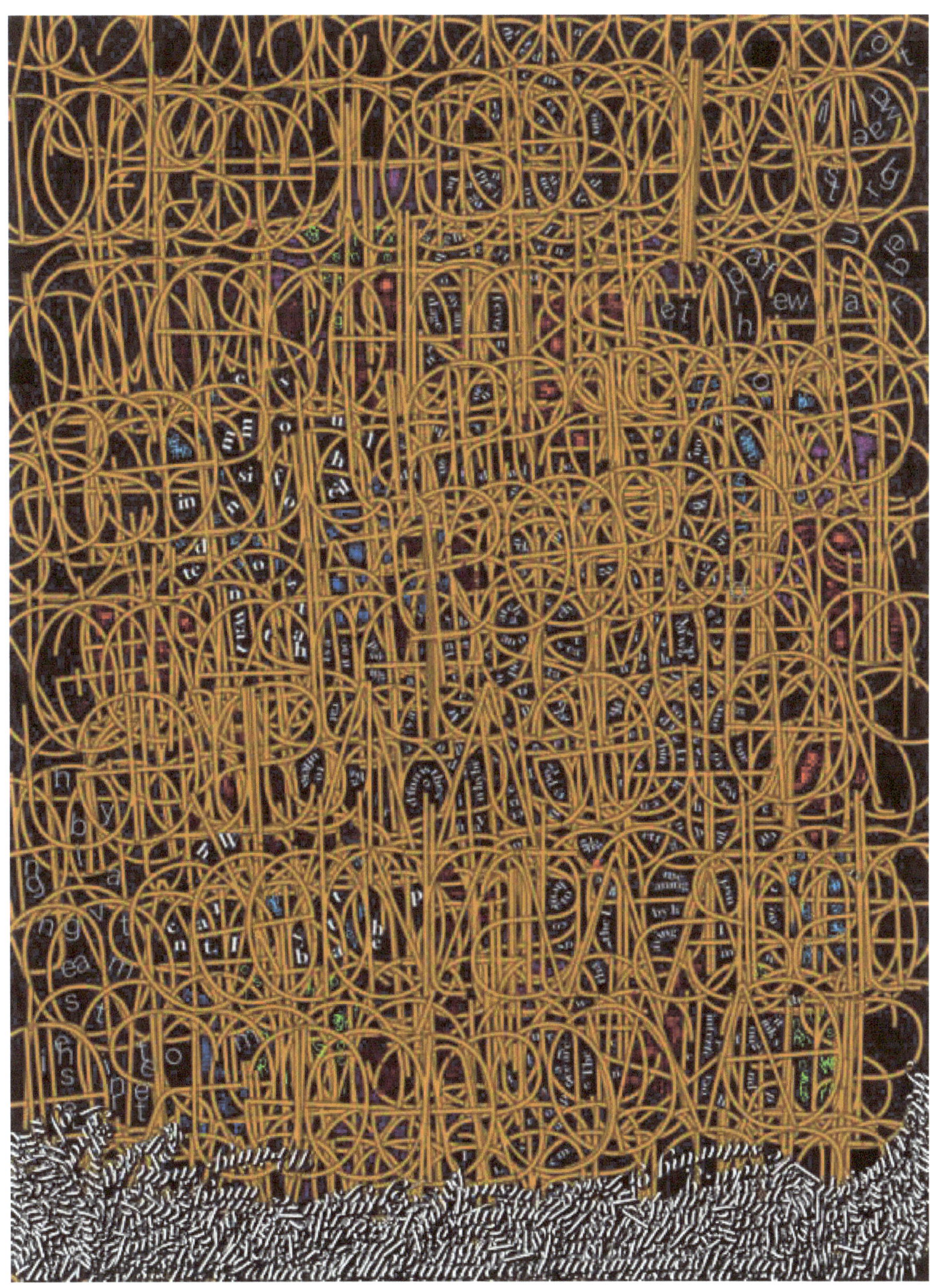

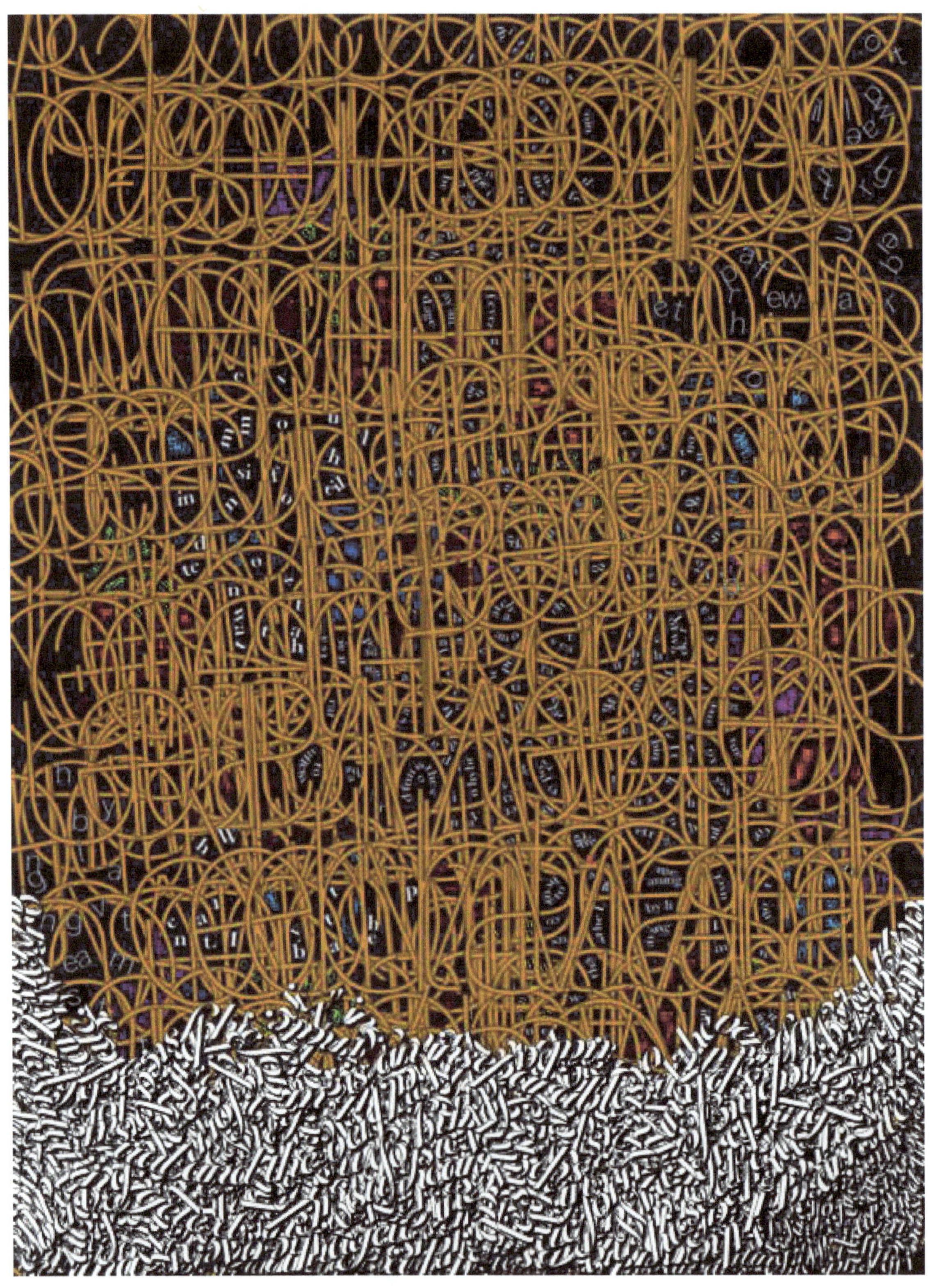

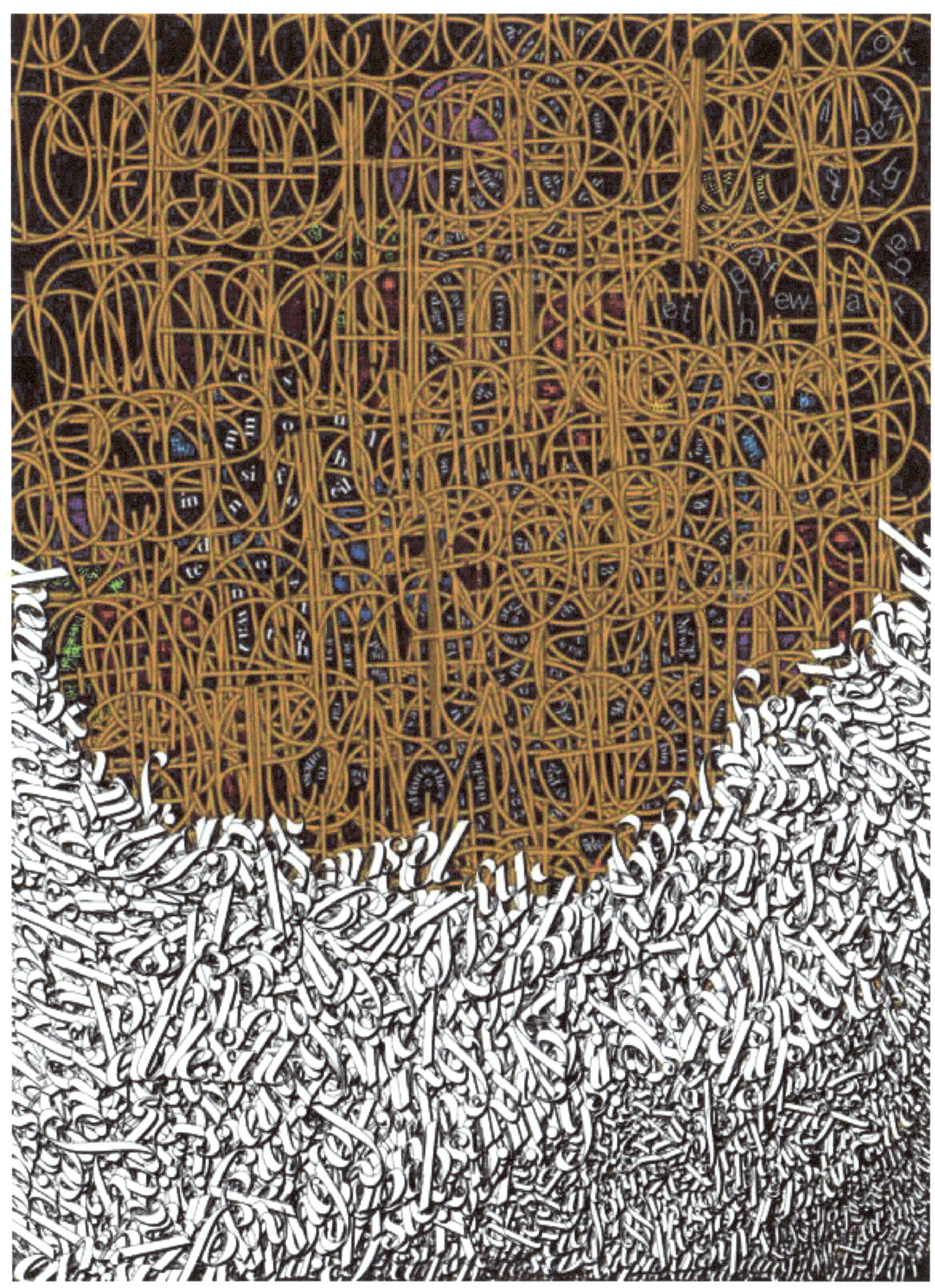

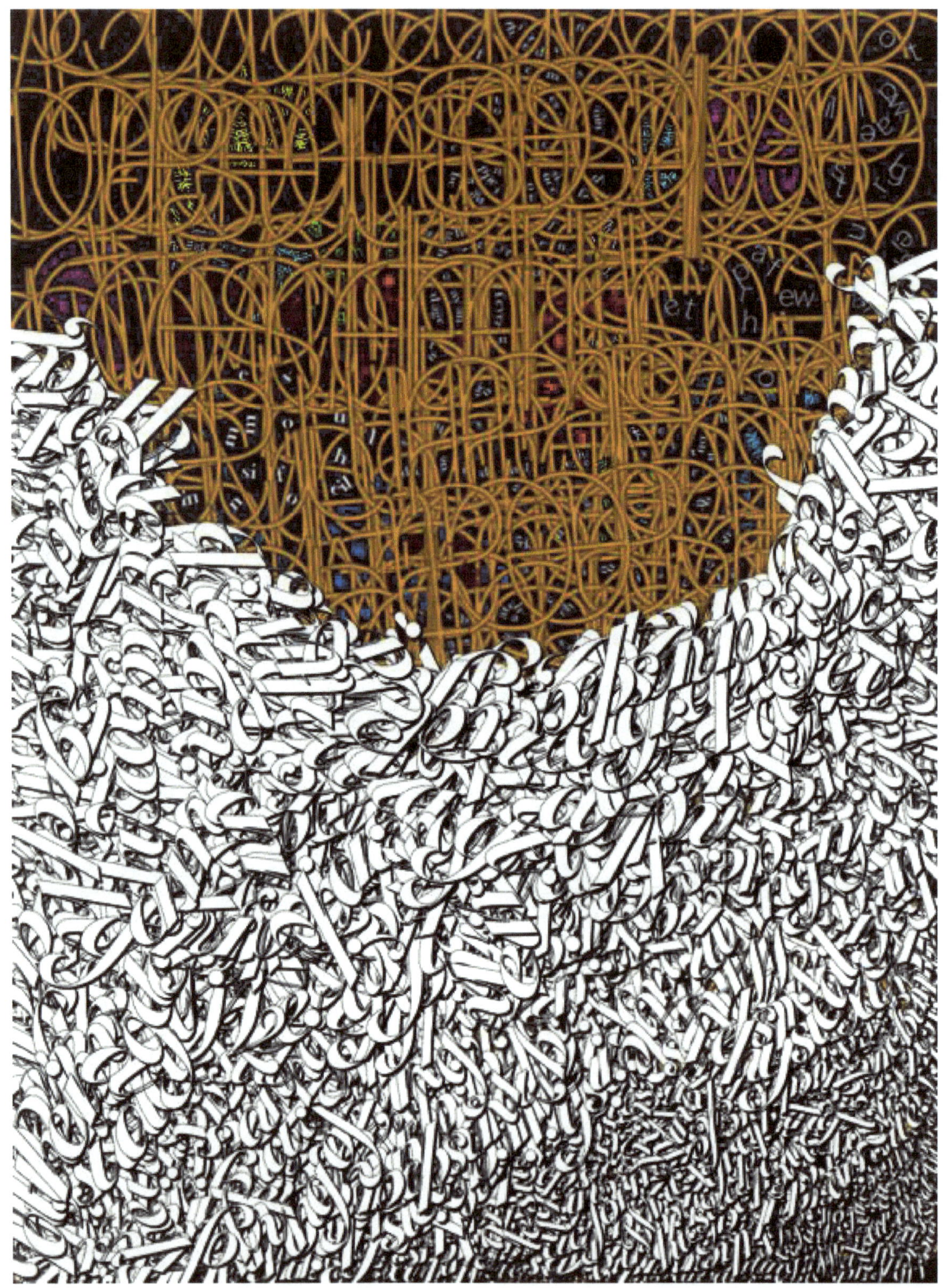

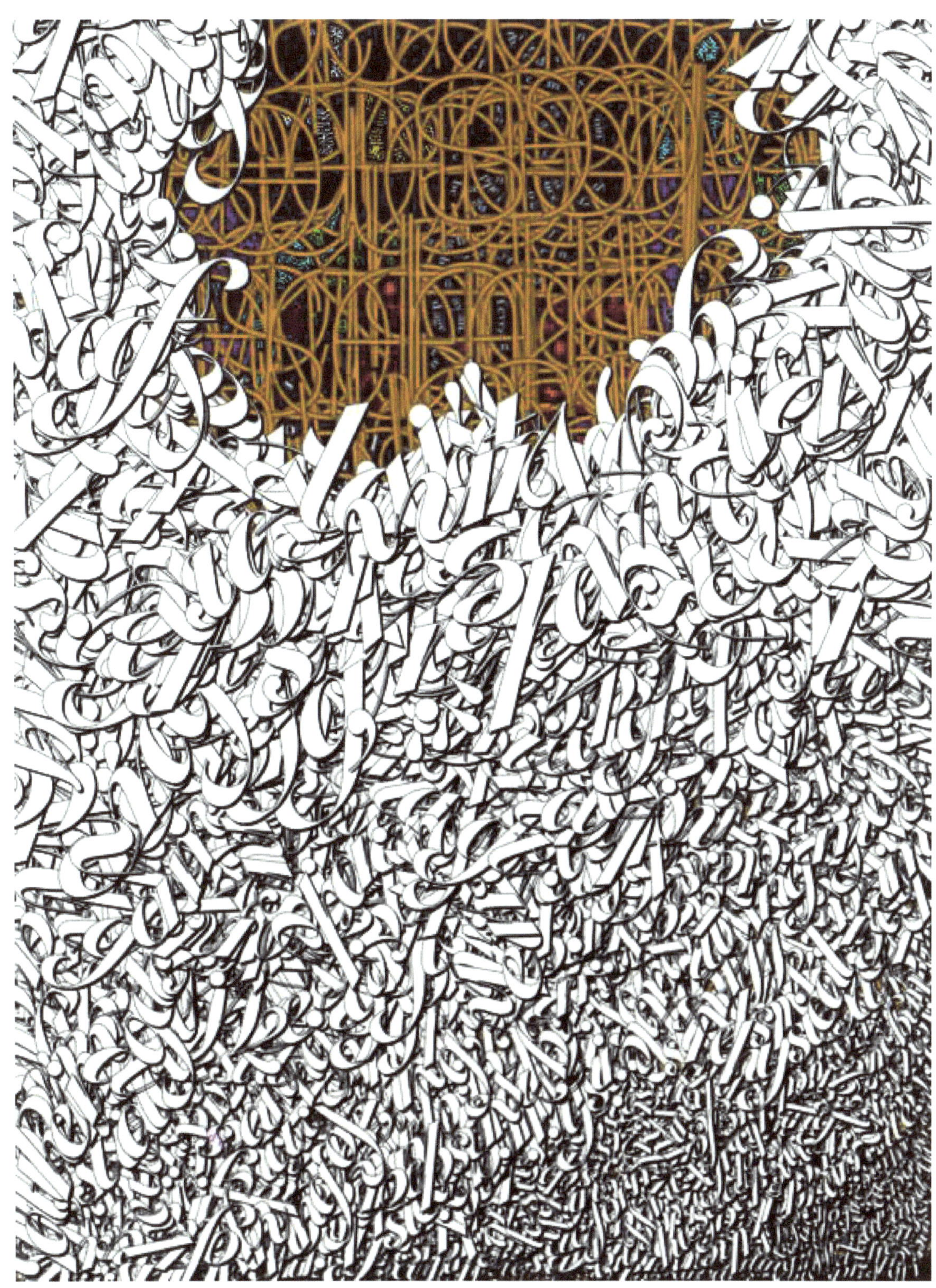

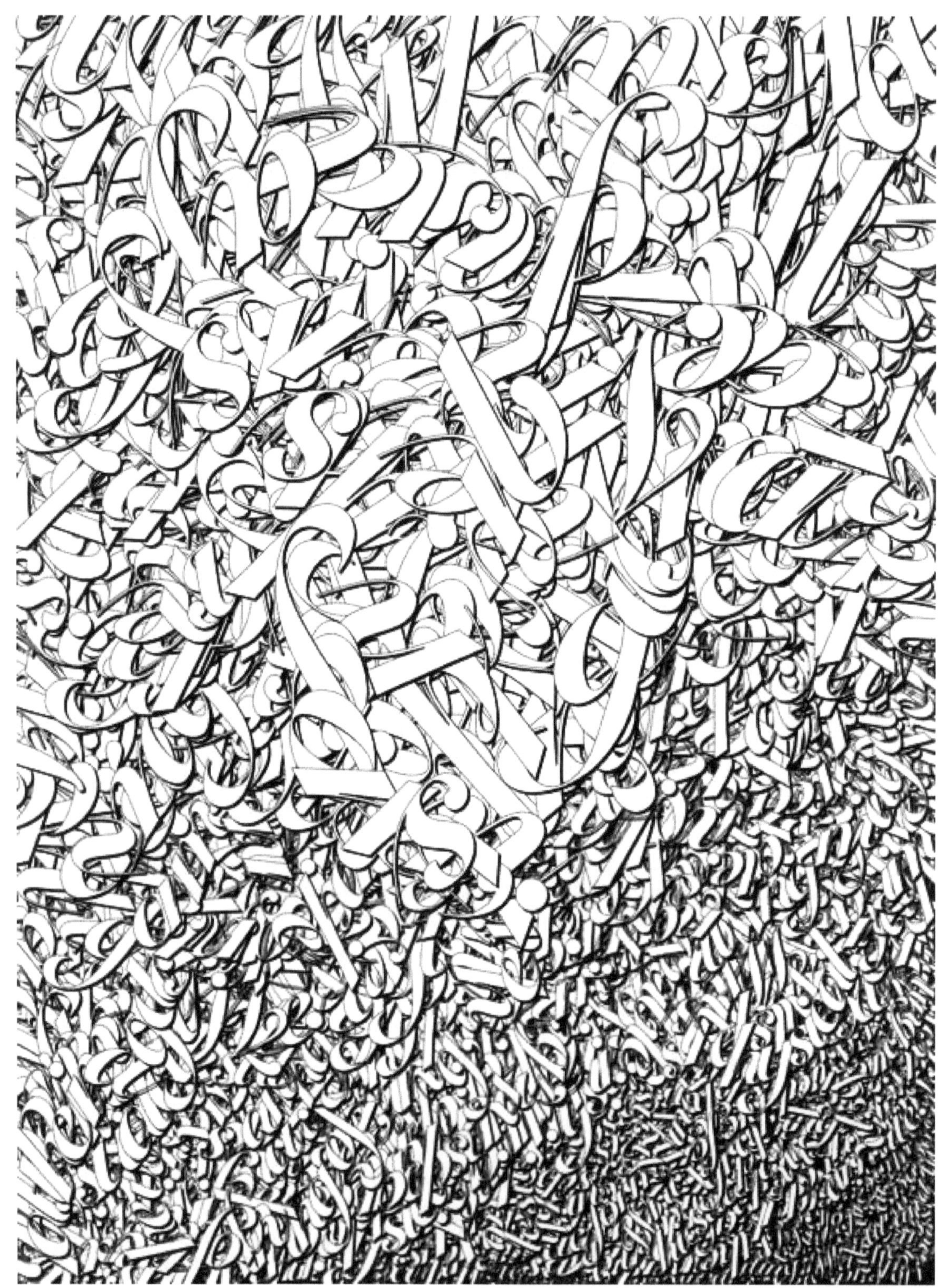

LETTERS ARE ESCAPING

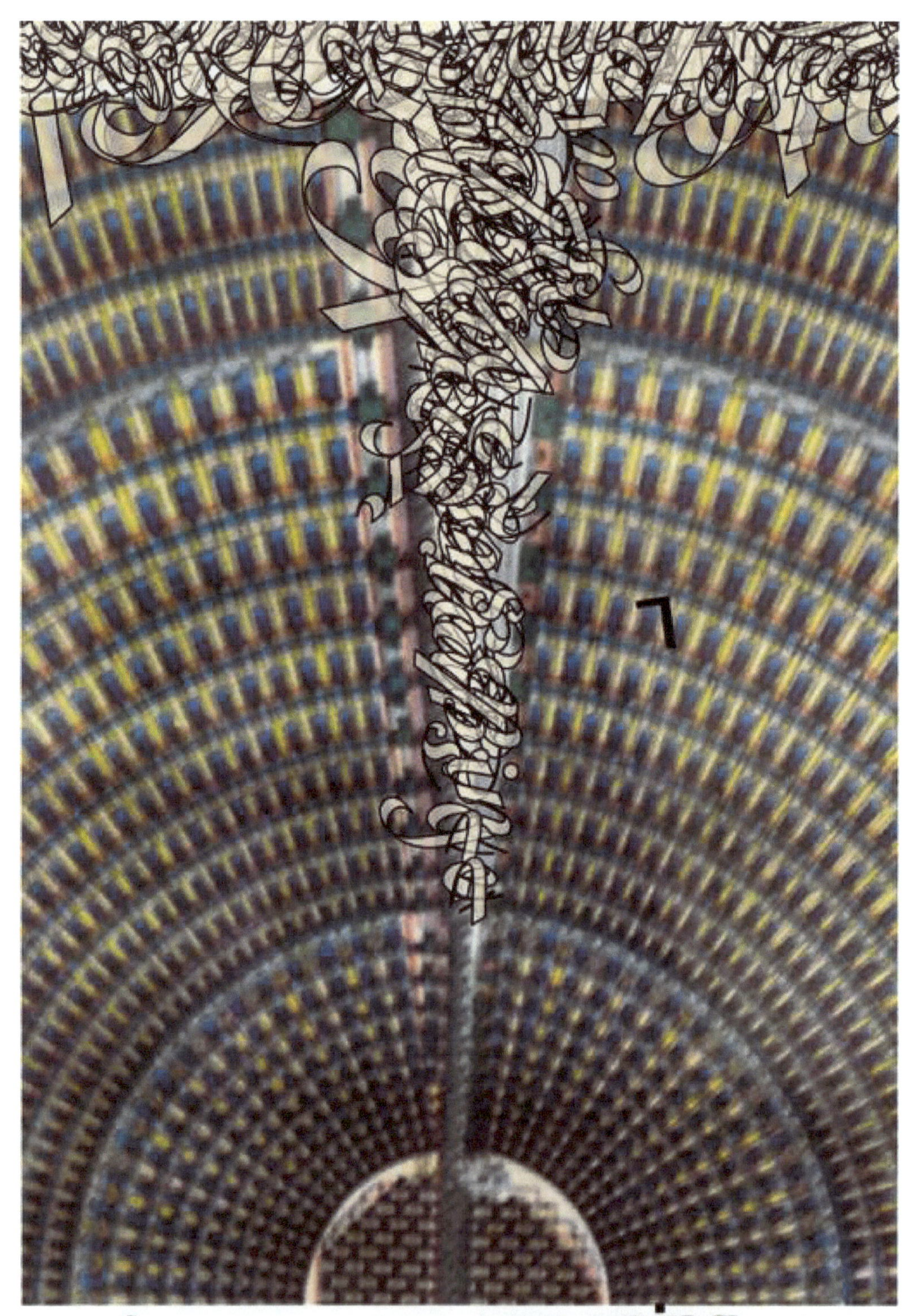

Letters are escaping

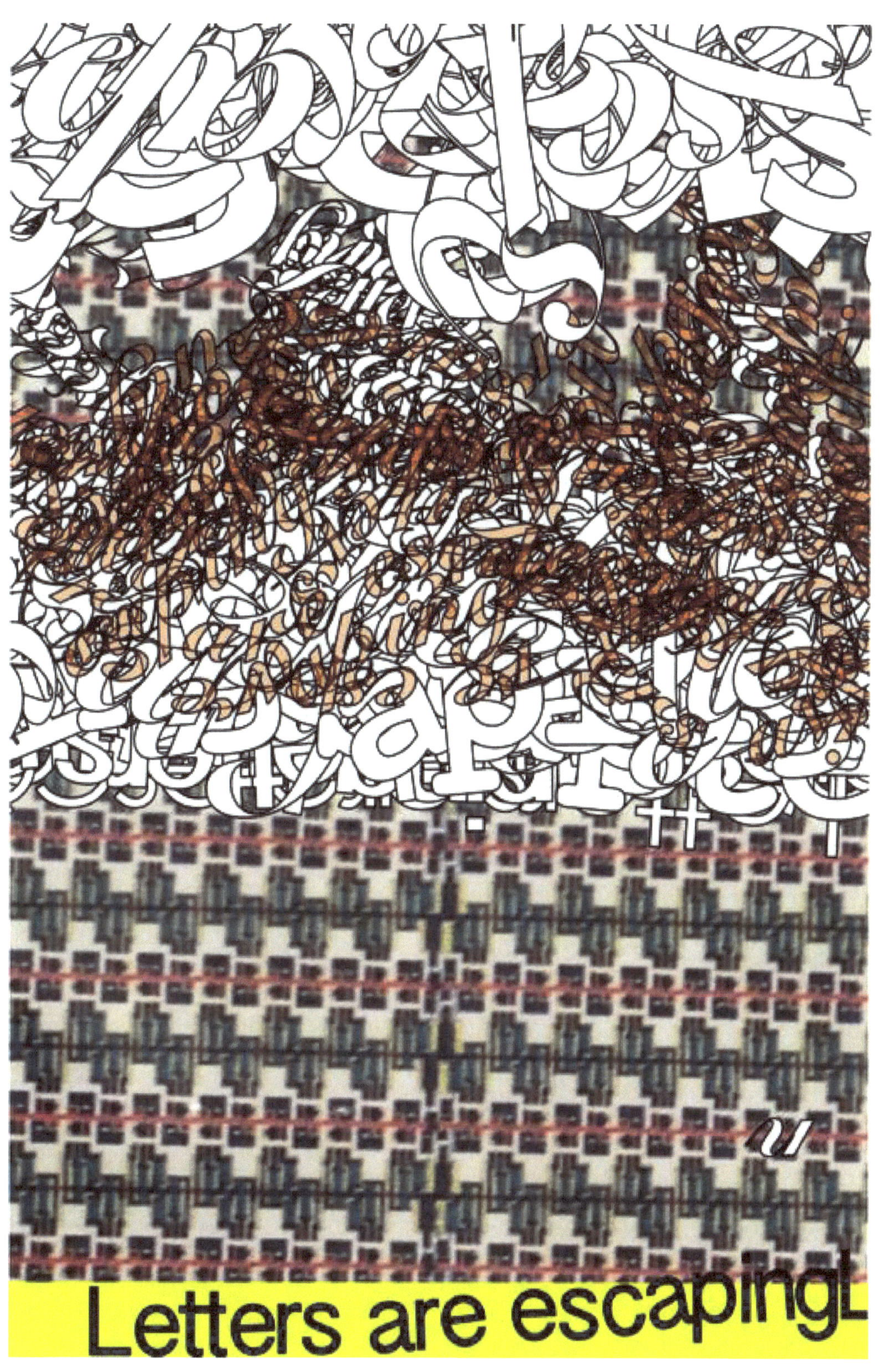

Letters are escaping!

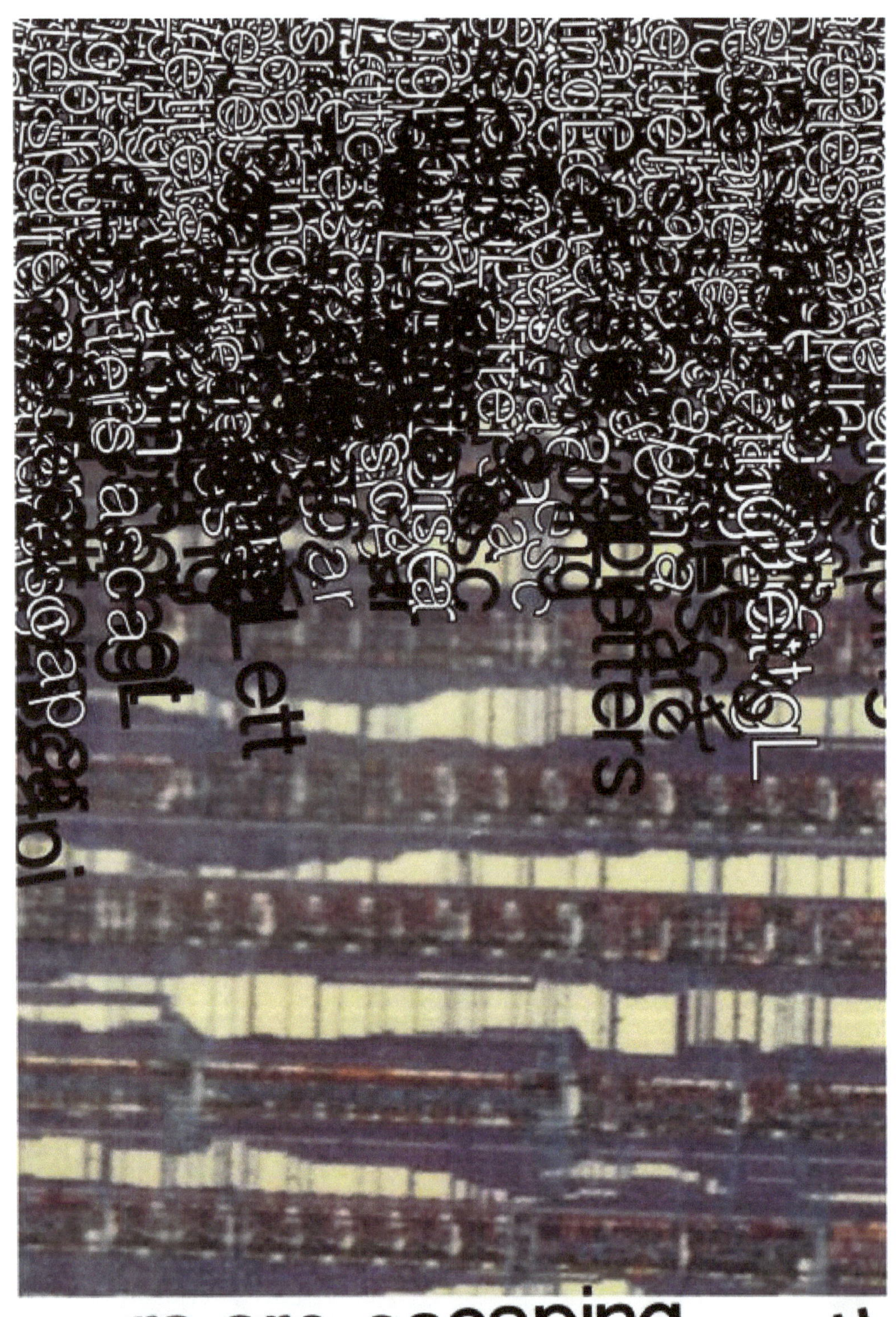
ers are escaping l ett

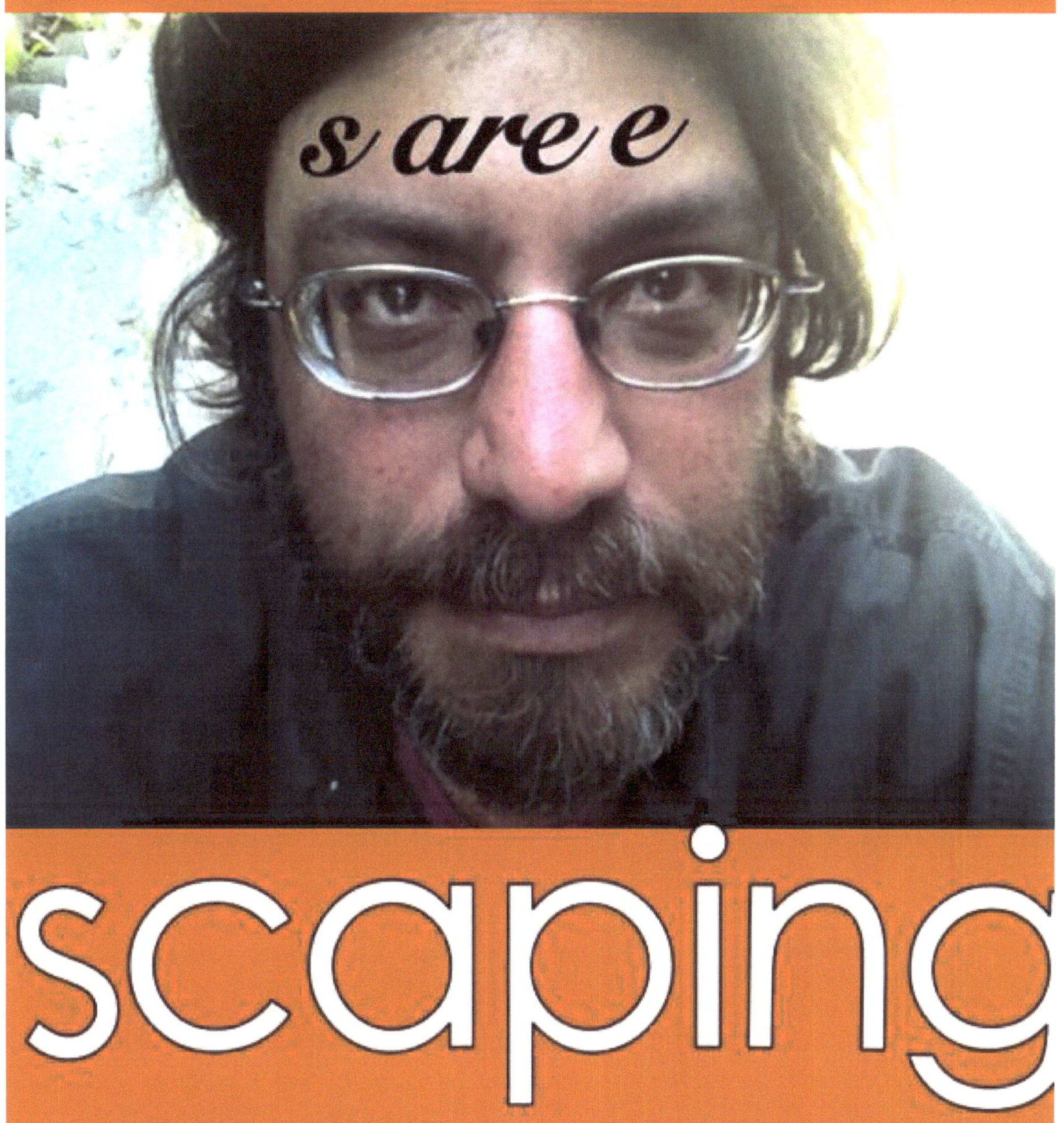

Letter
s are e
scaping

MANIFESTO

words
are
letter
comb
ination
s

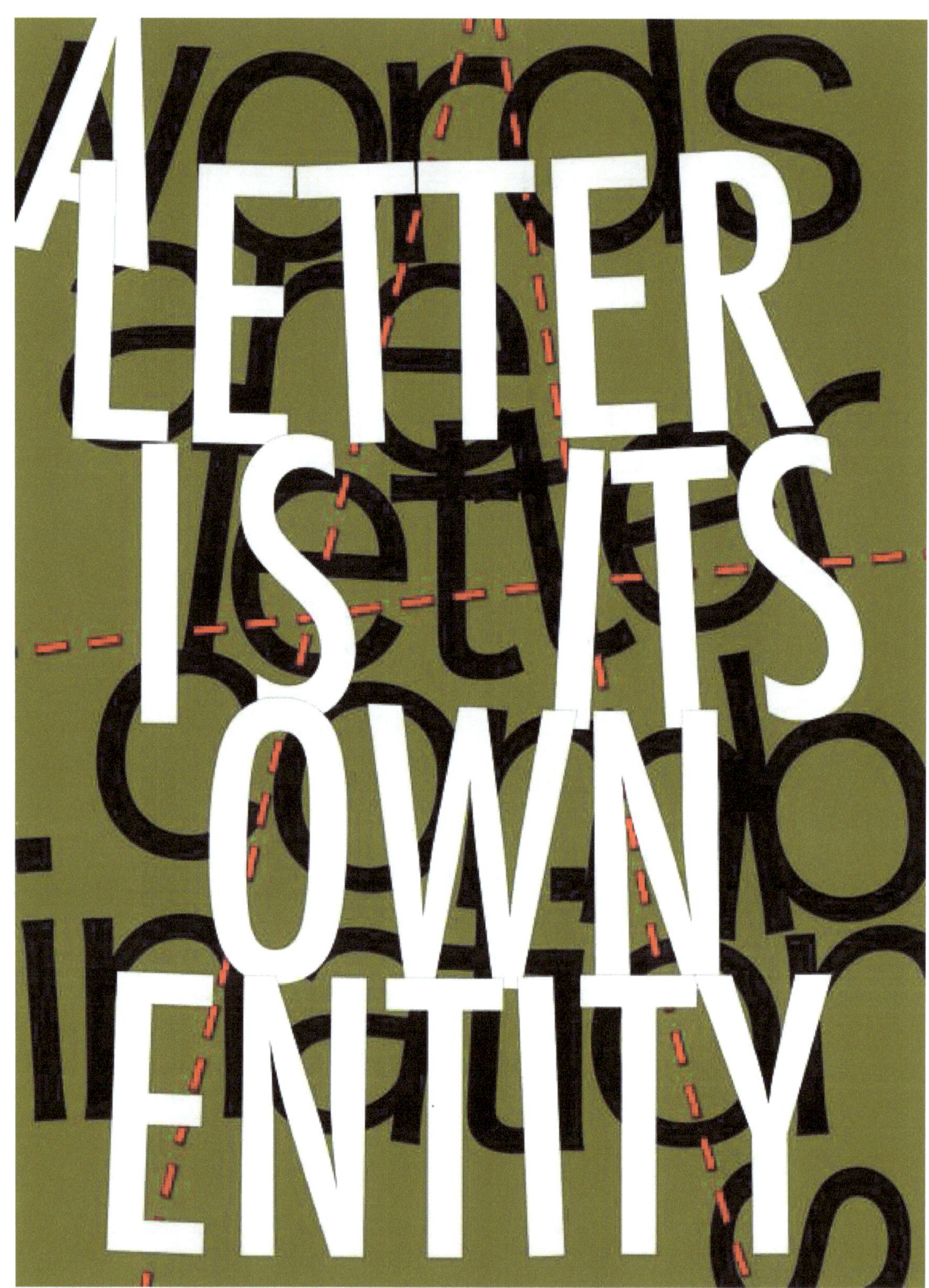

LETTER
IS ITS
OWN
ENTITY

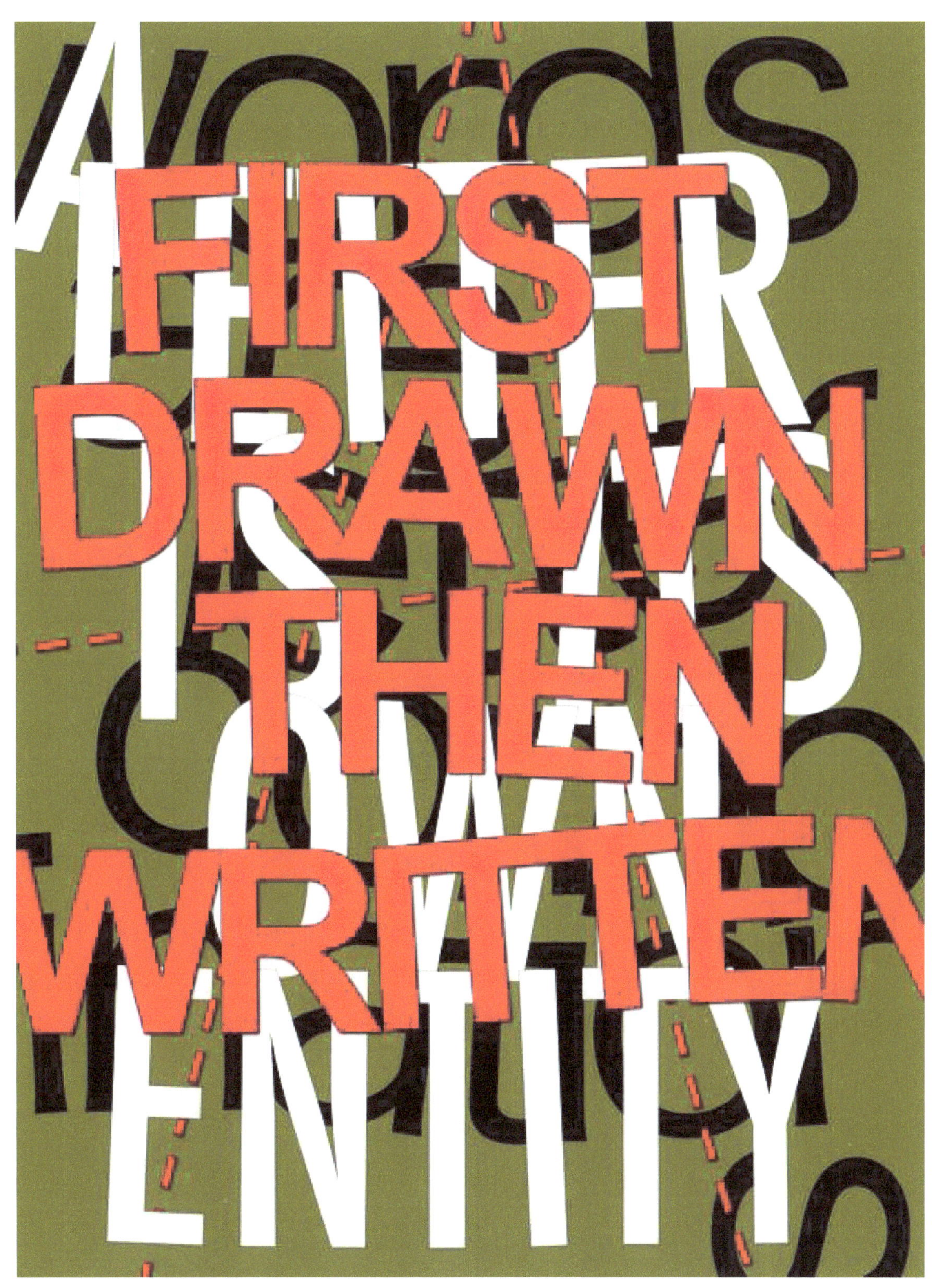
Words
FIRST
DRAWN
THEN
WRITTEN
ENTITY

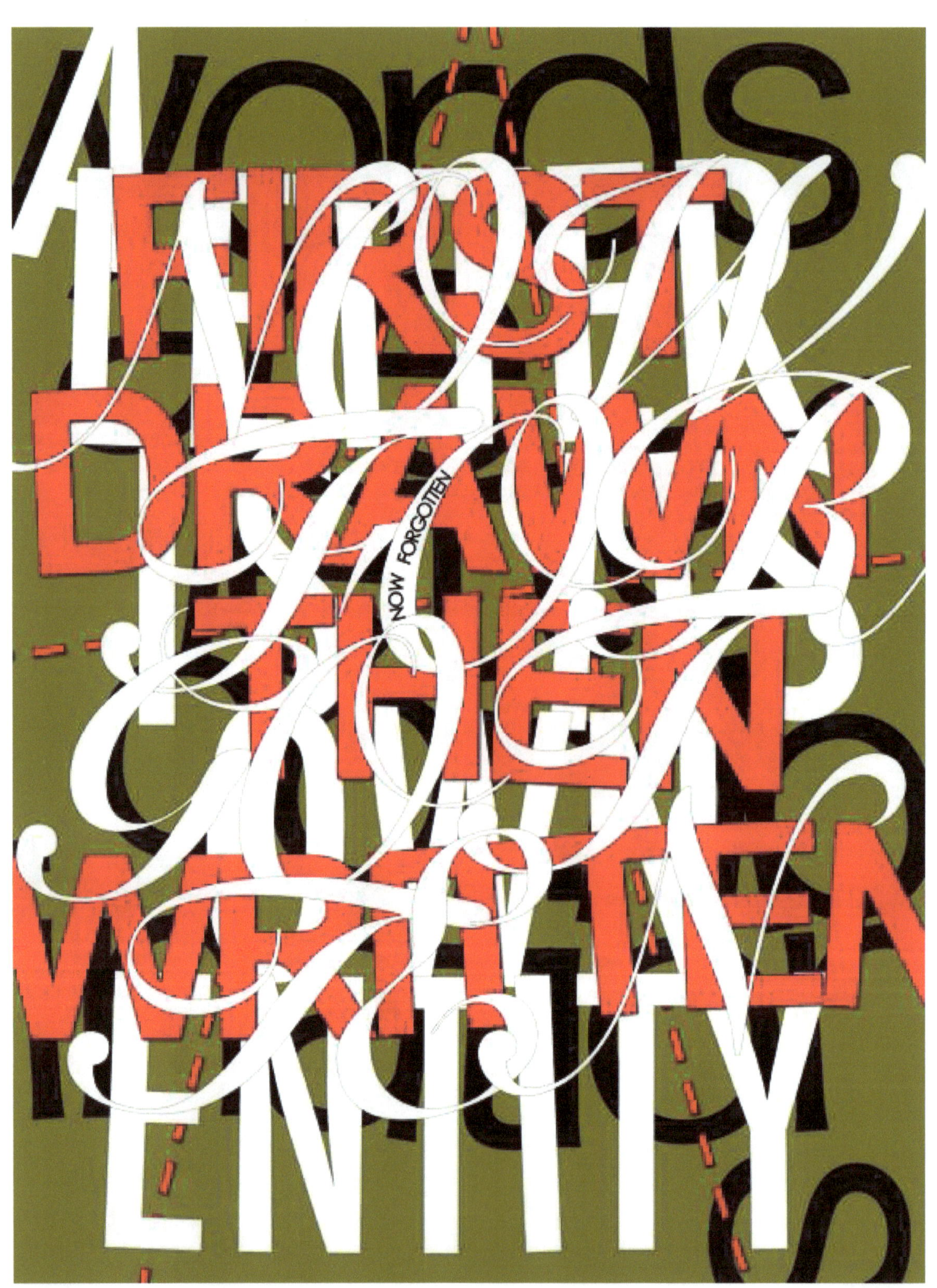
NOW FORGOTTEN

ONE METHOD

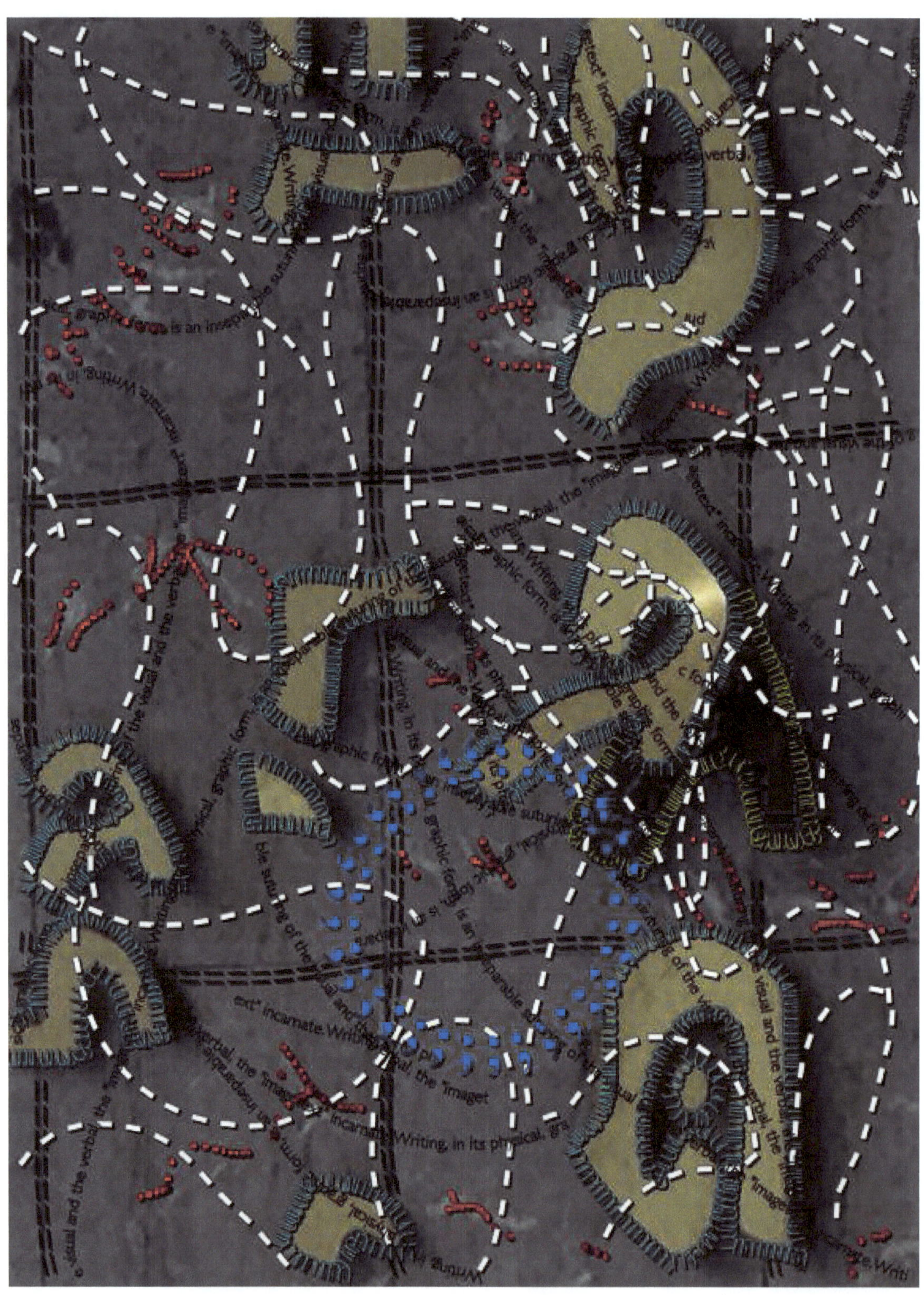

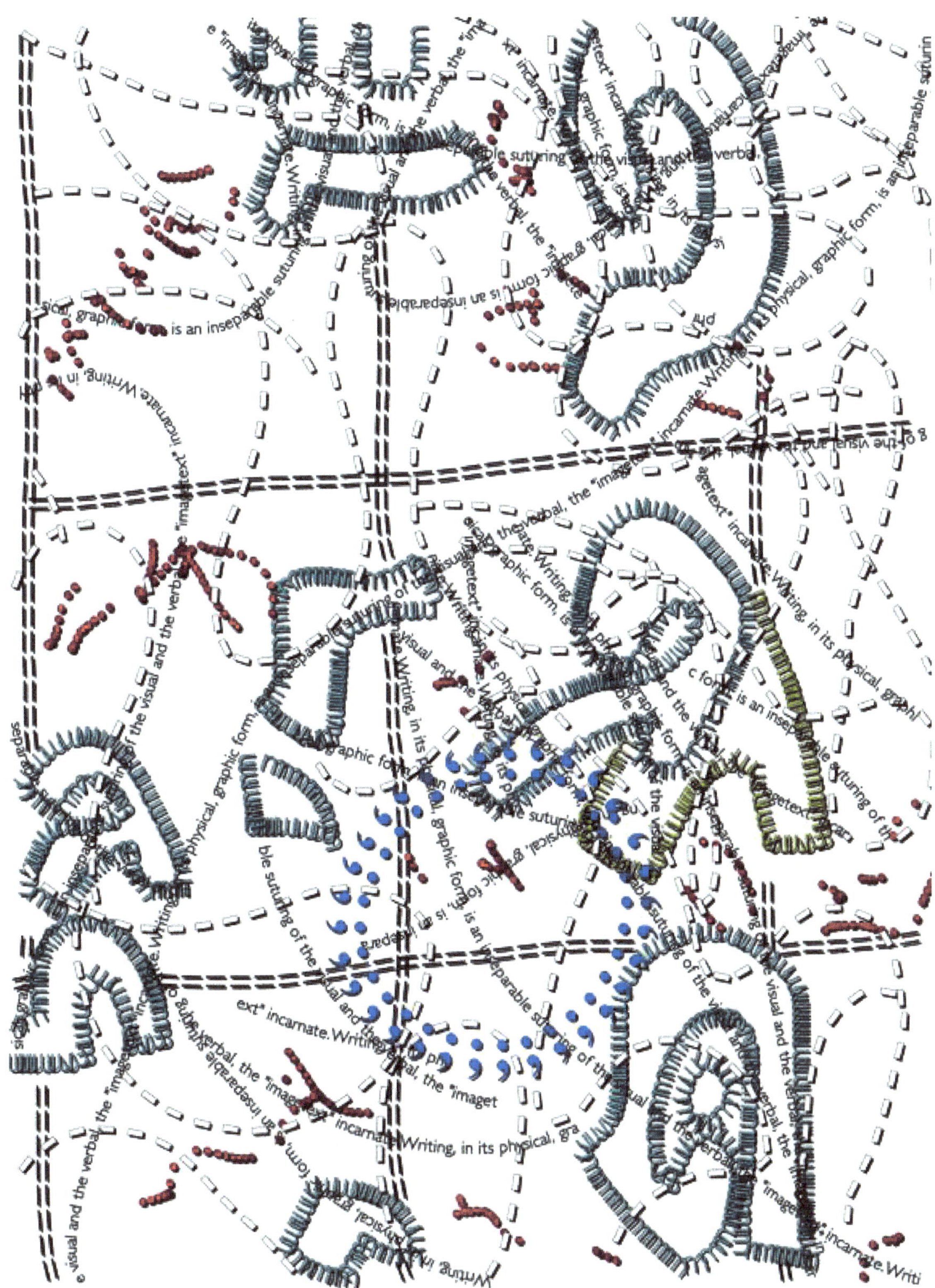

TWO METHOD

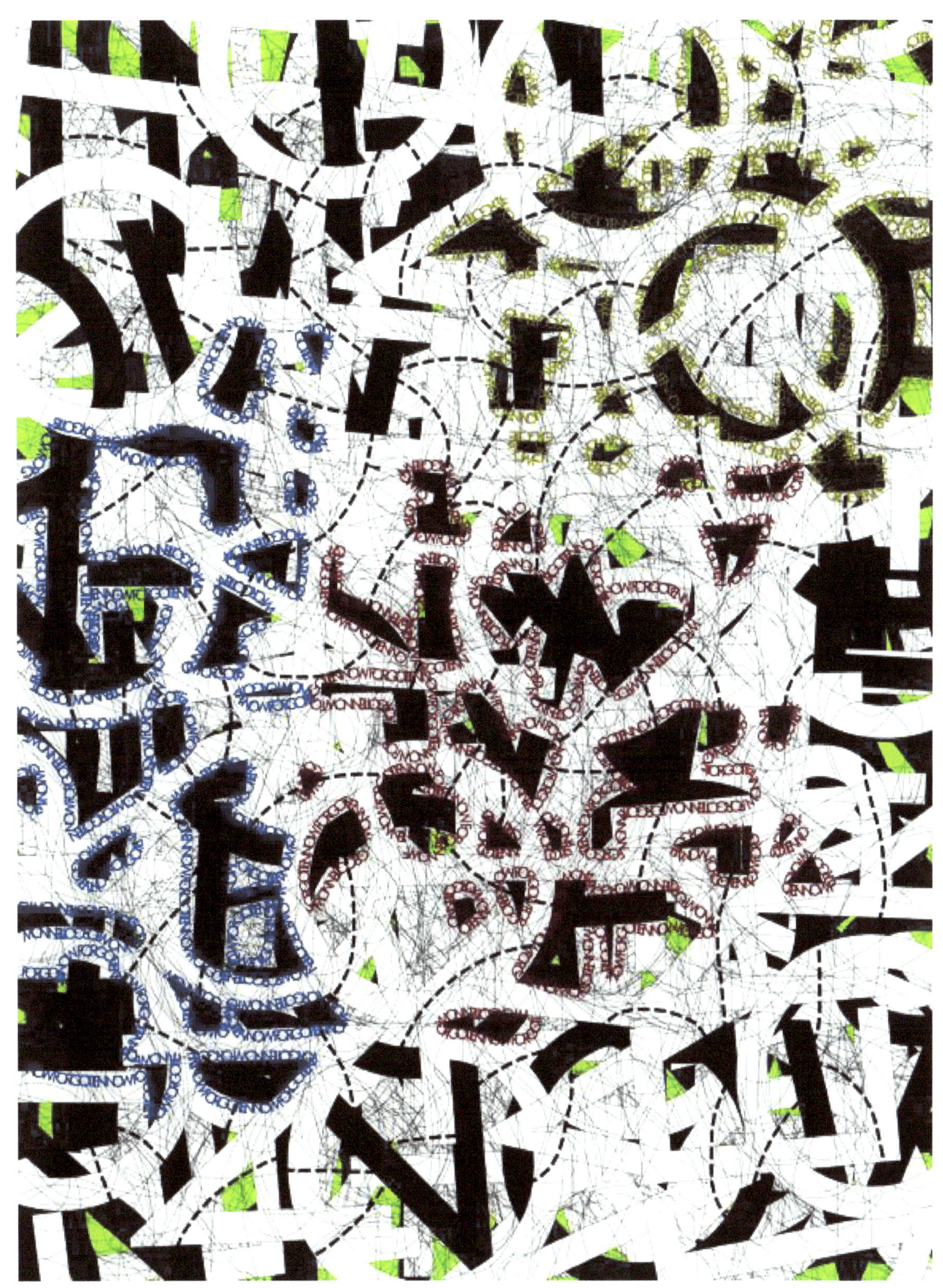

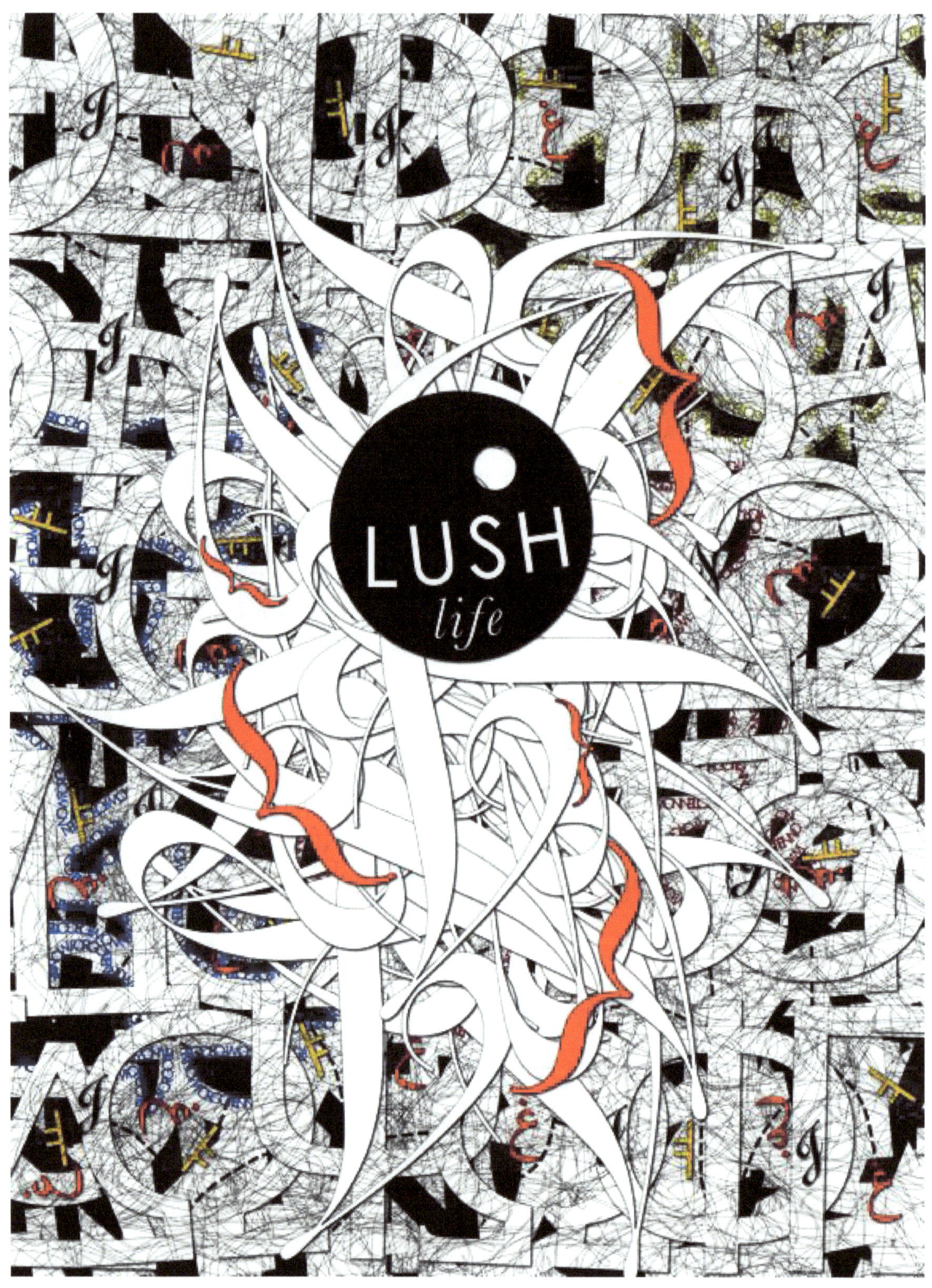

LUSH
life

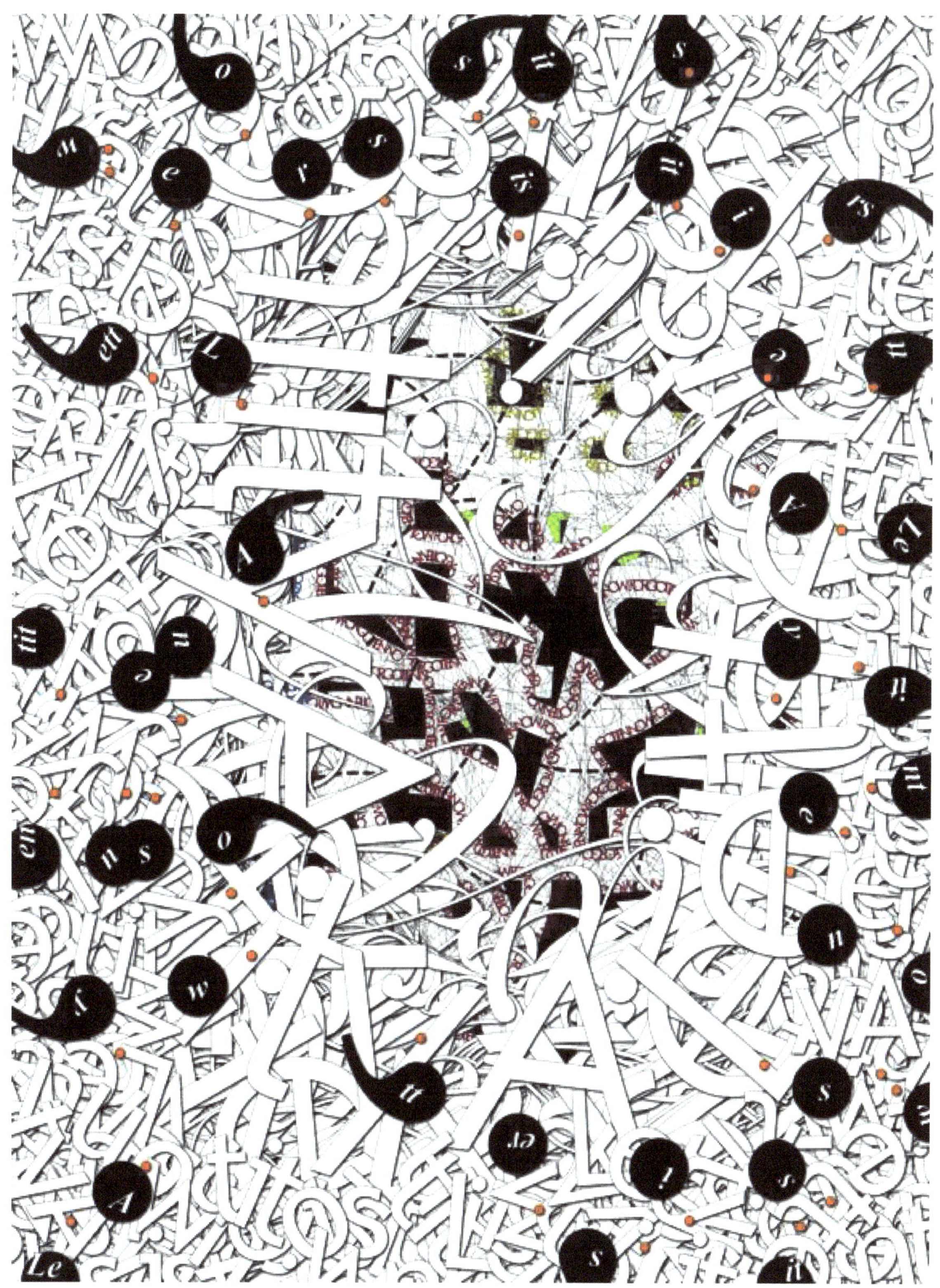

THREE METHOD

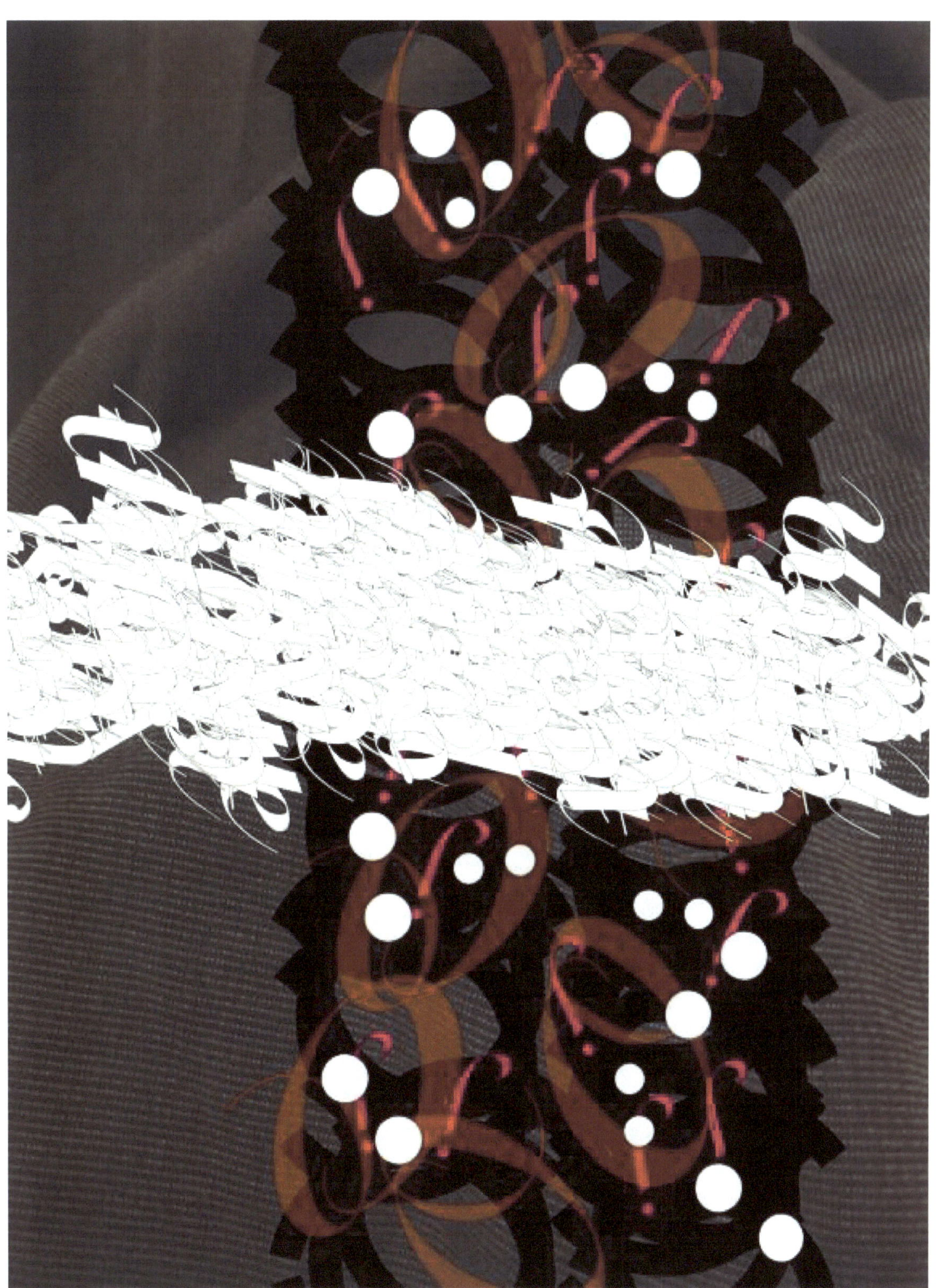

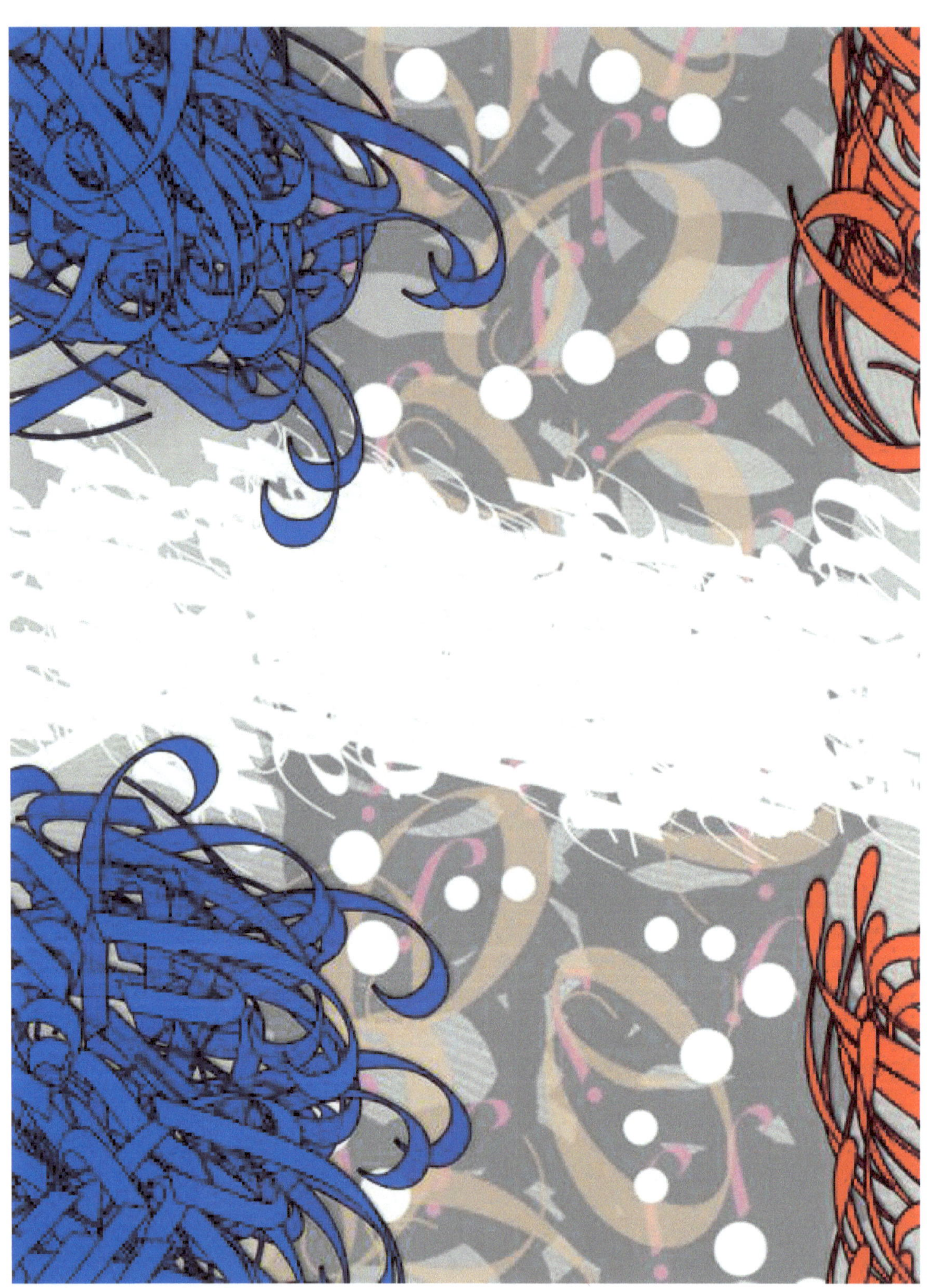

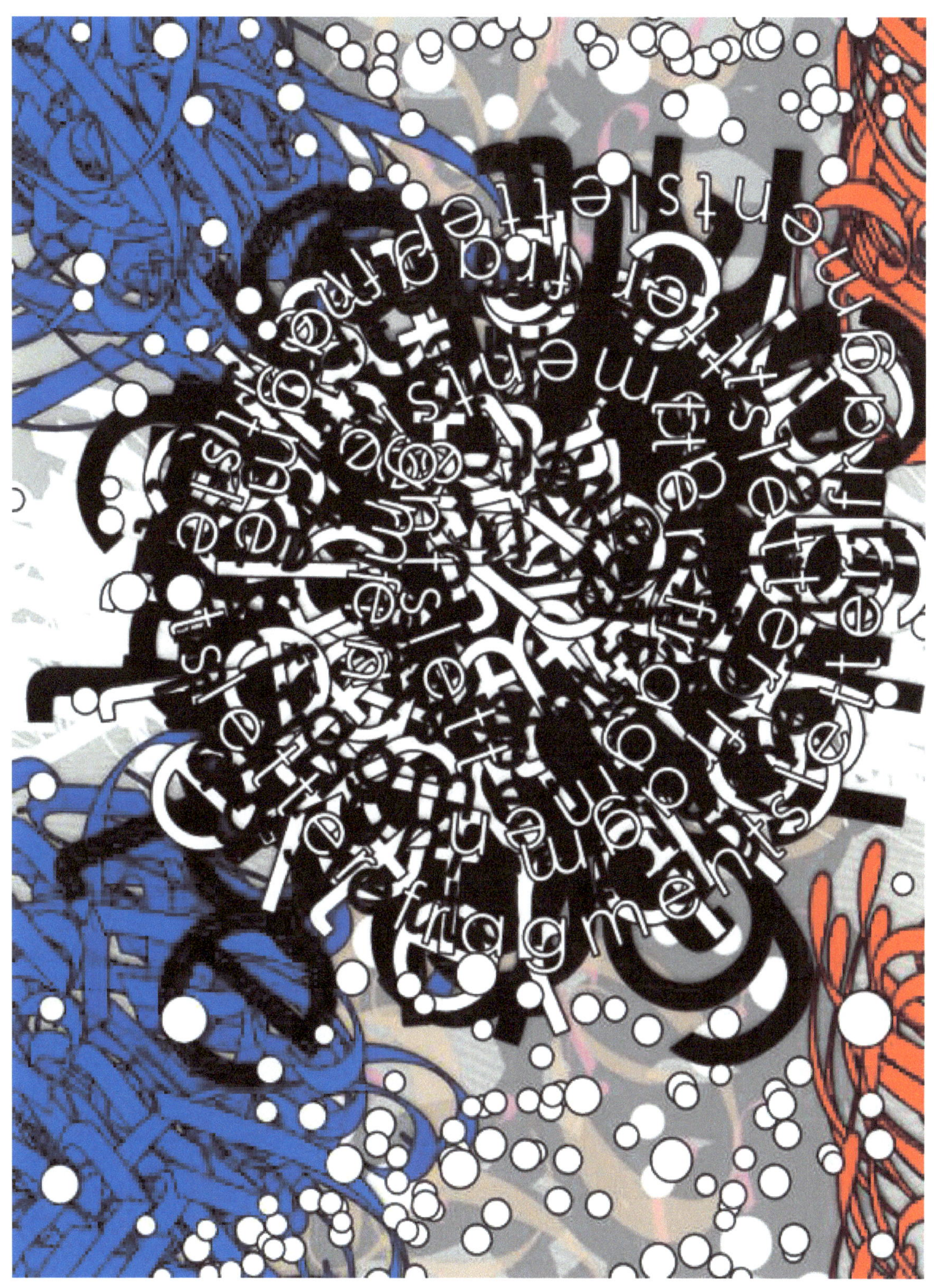

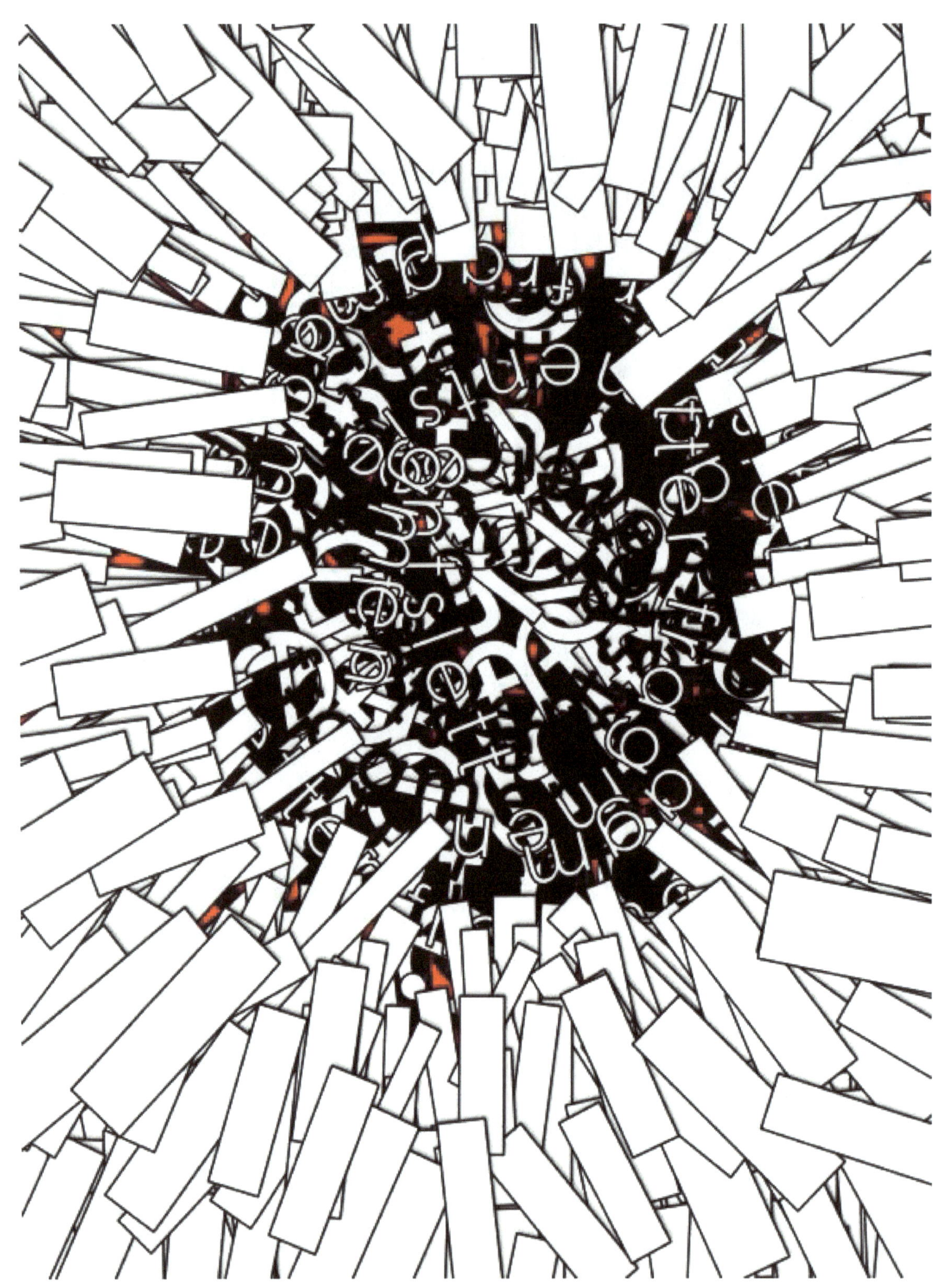

TEXT PICTURE

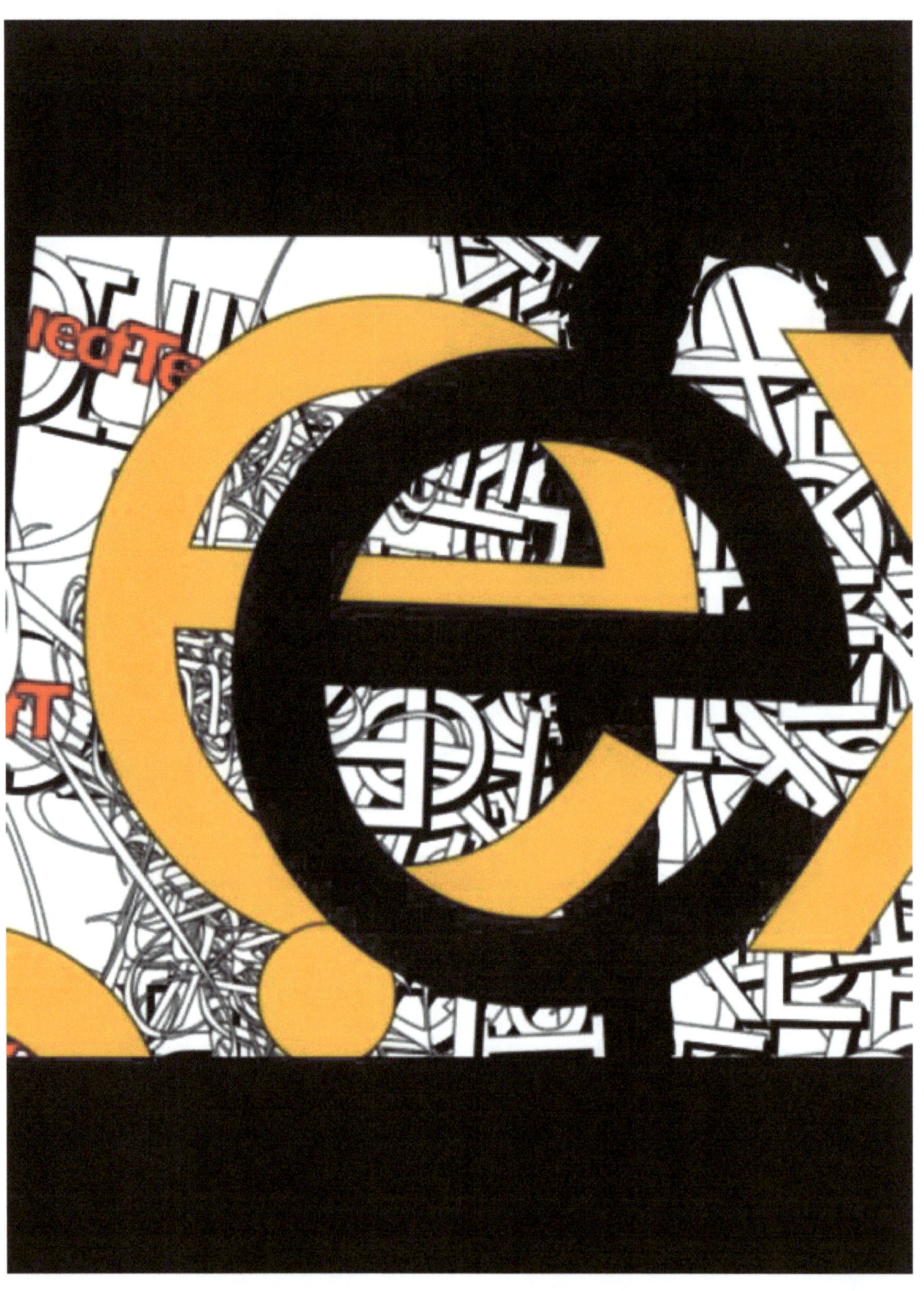

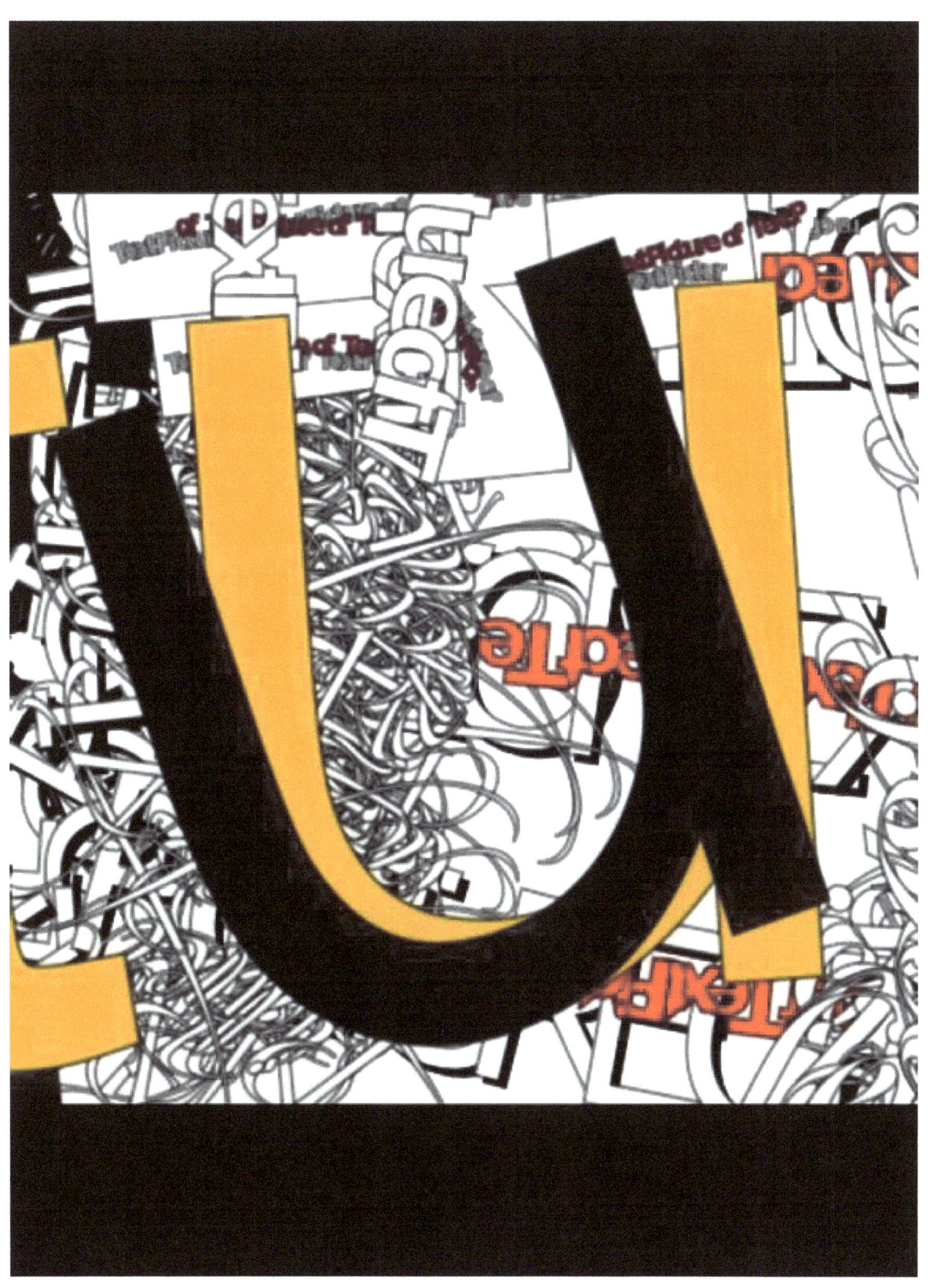

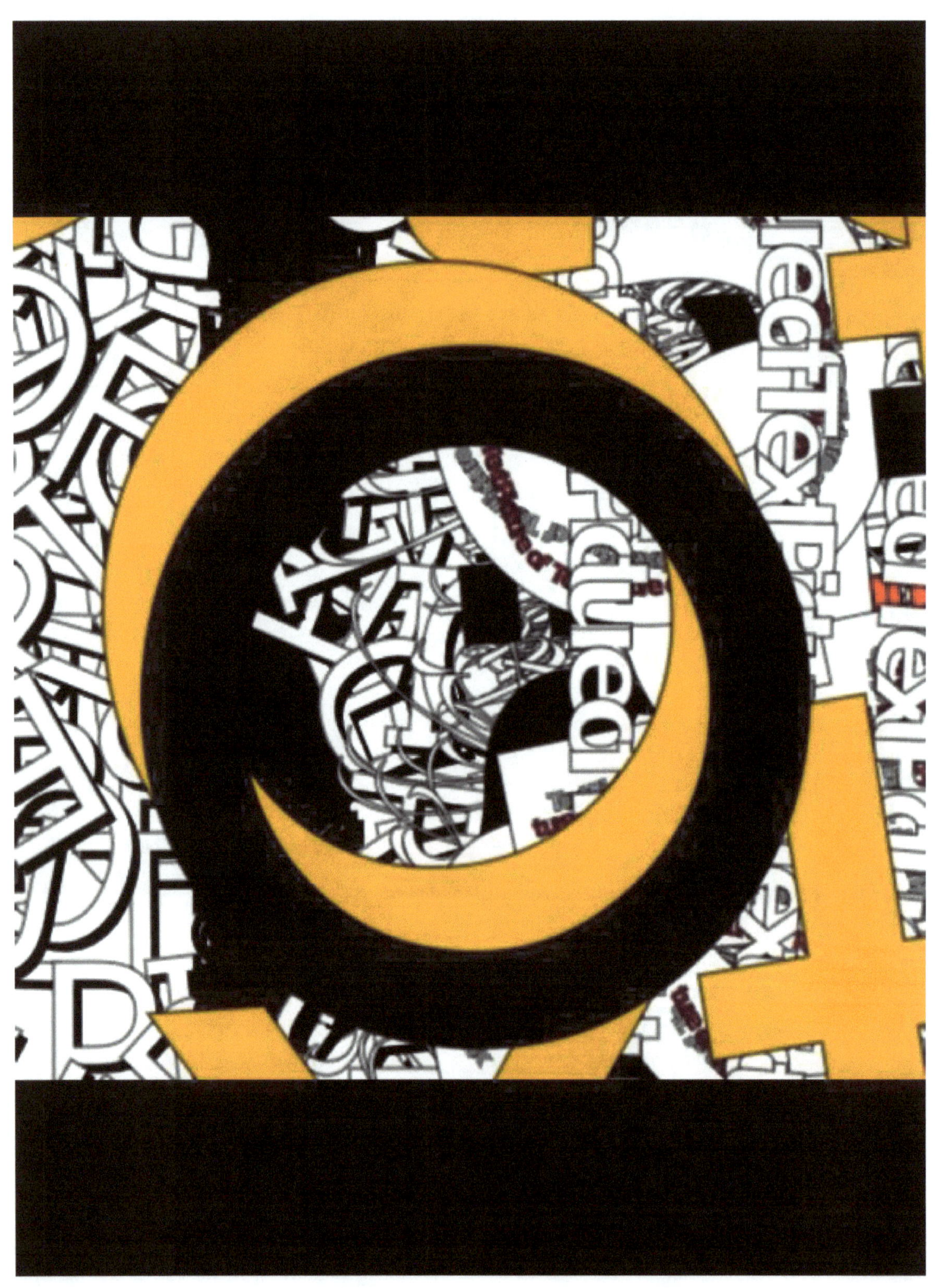

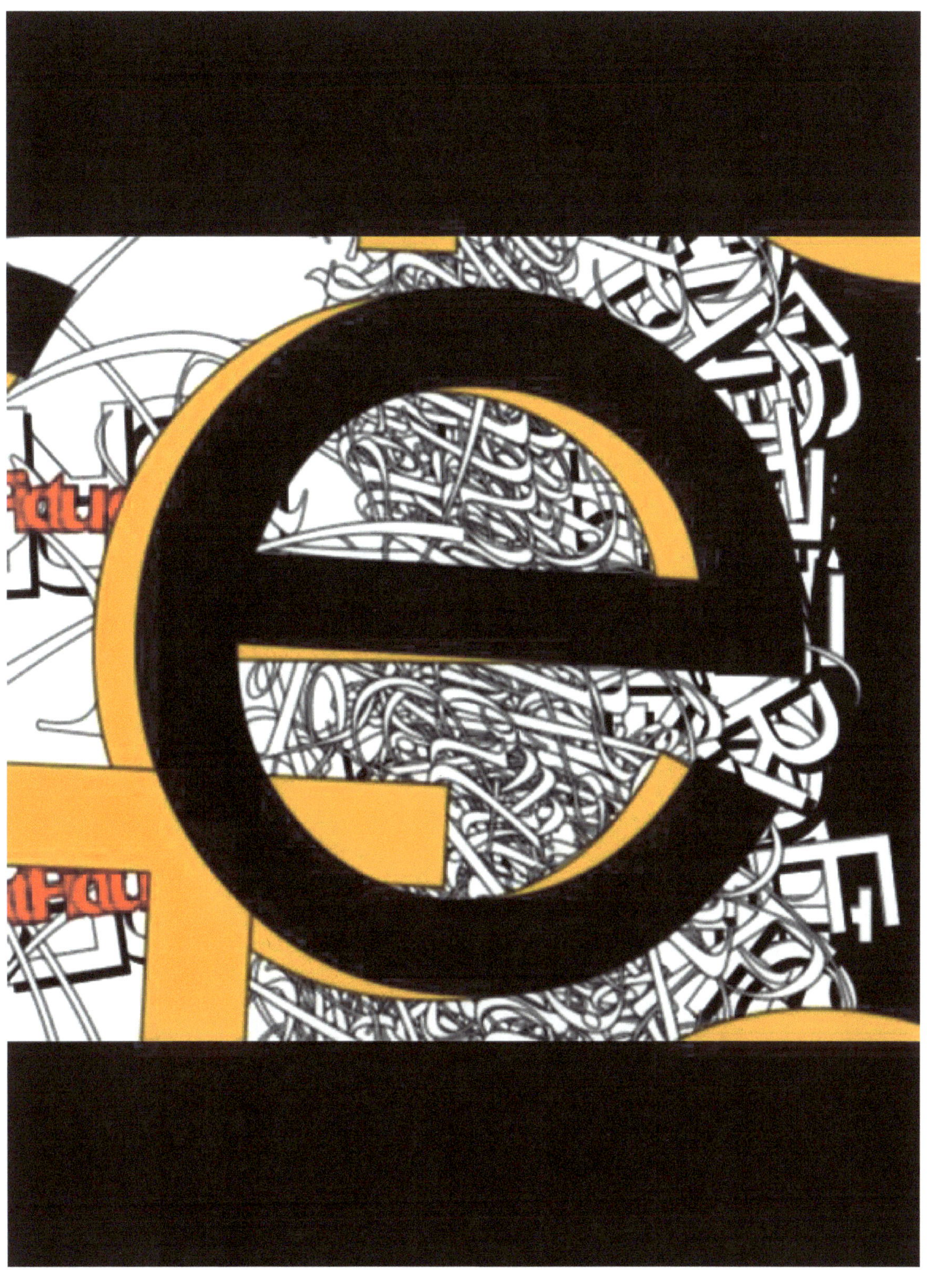

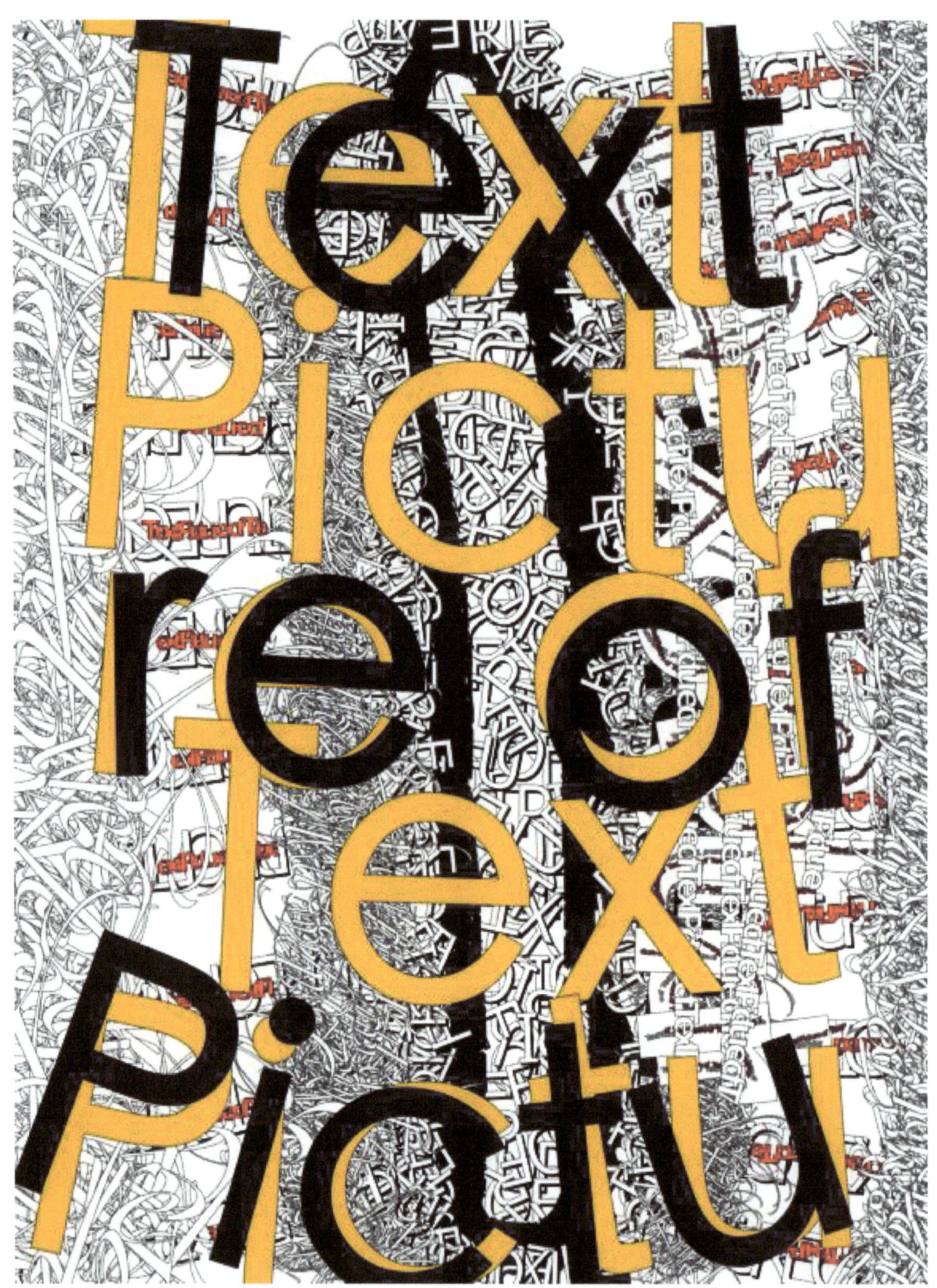

GENERATING/ELIMINATING

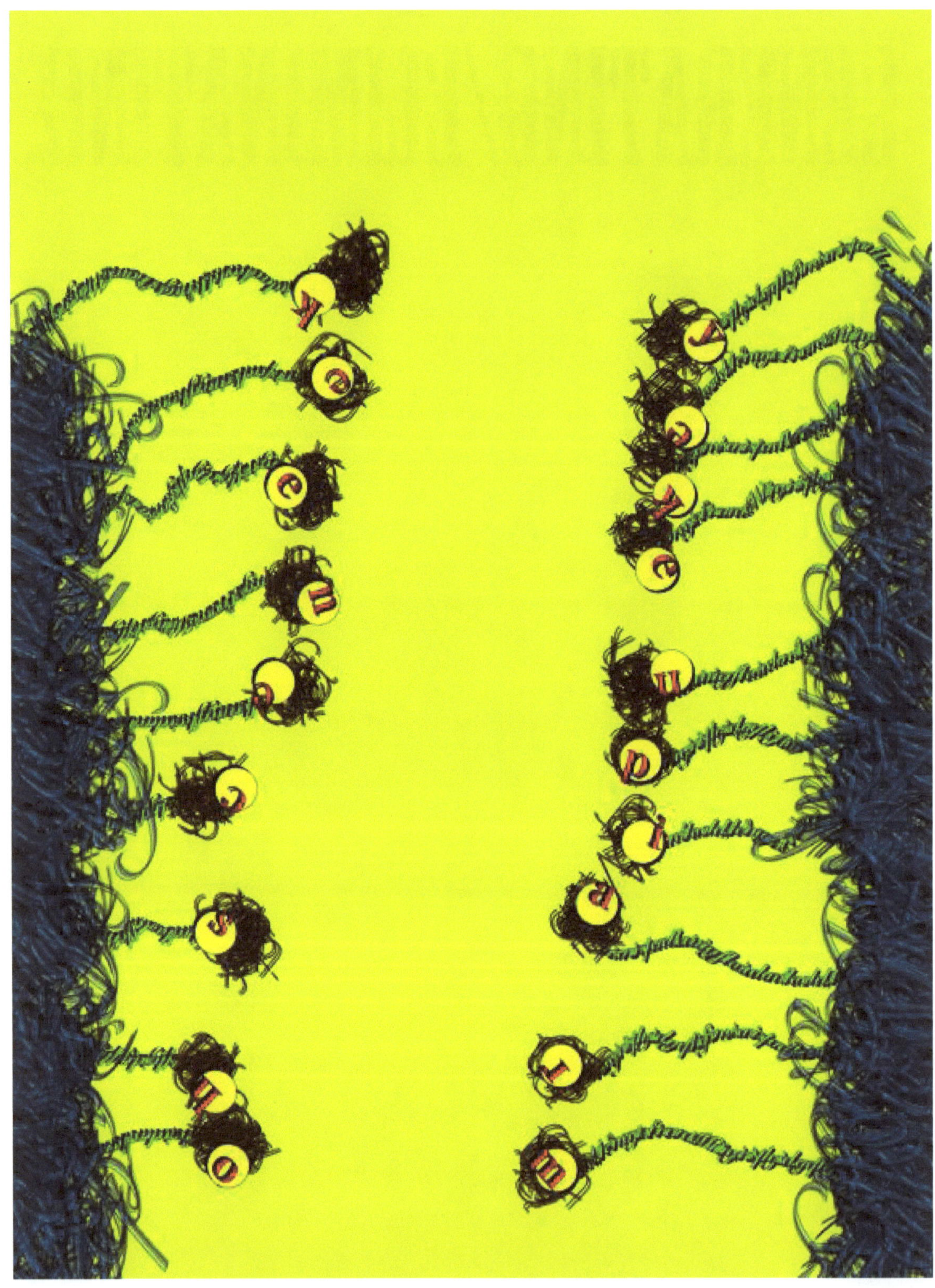

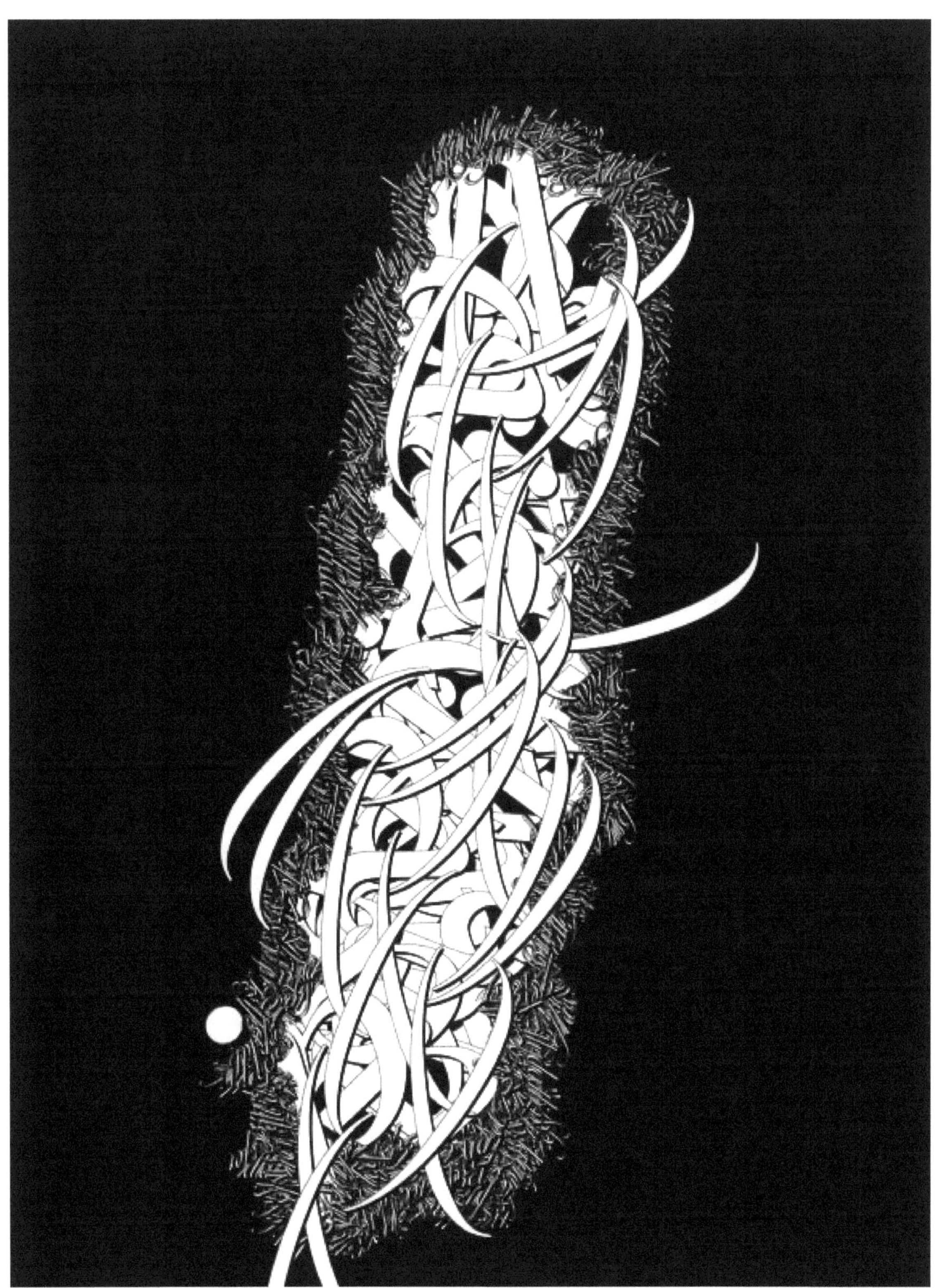

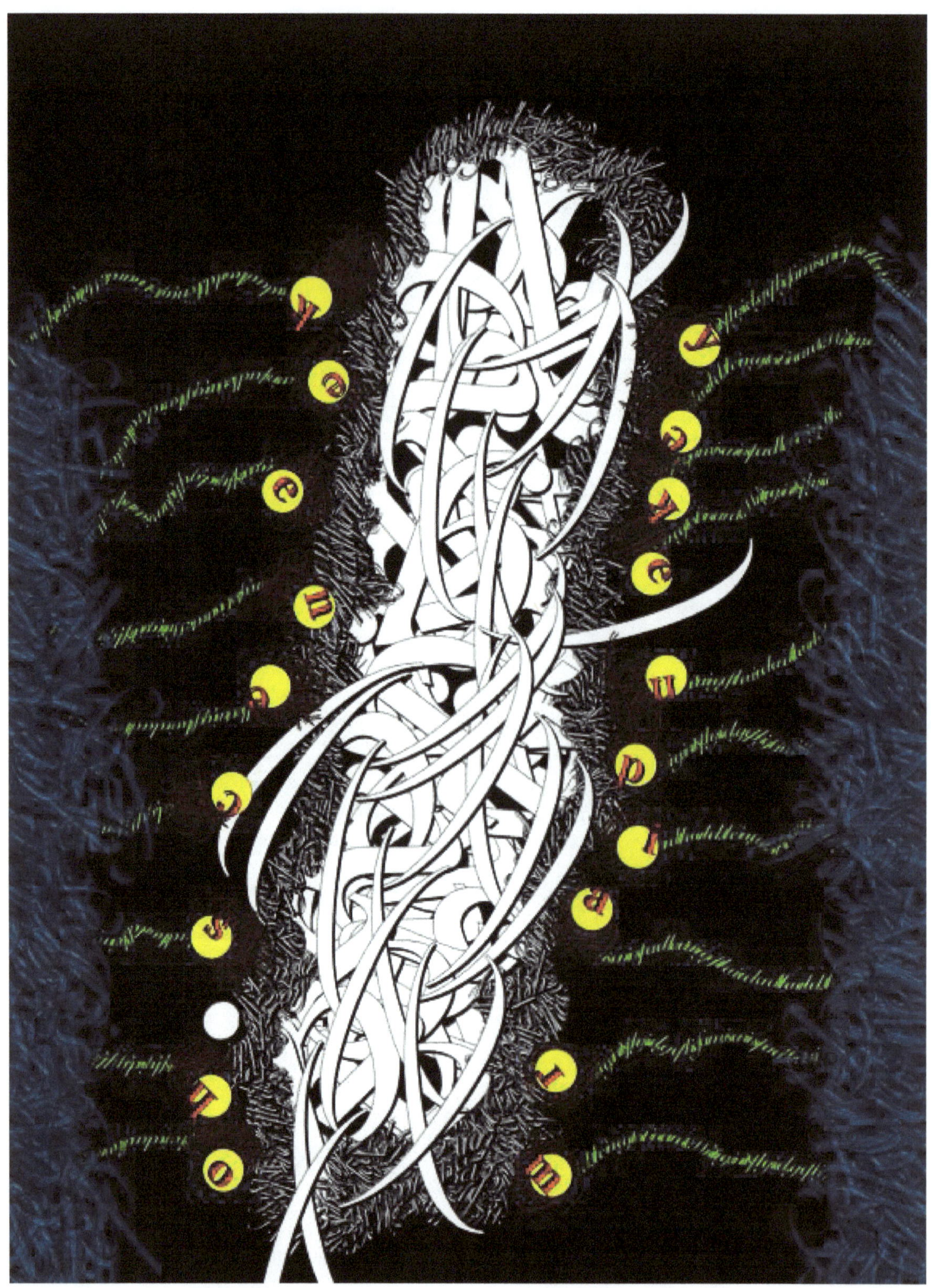

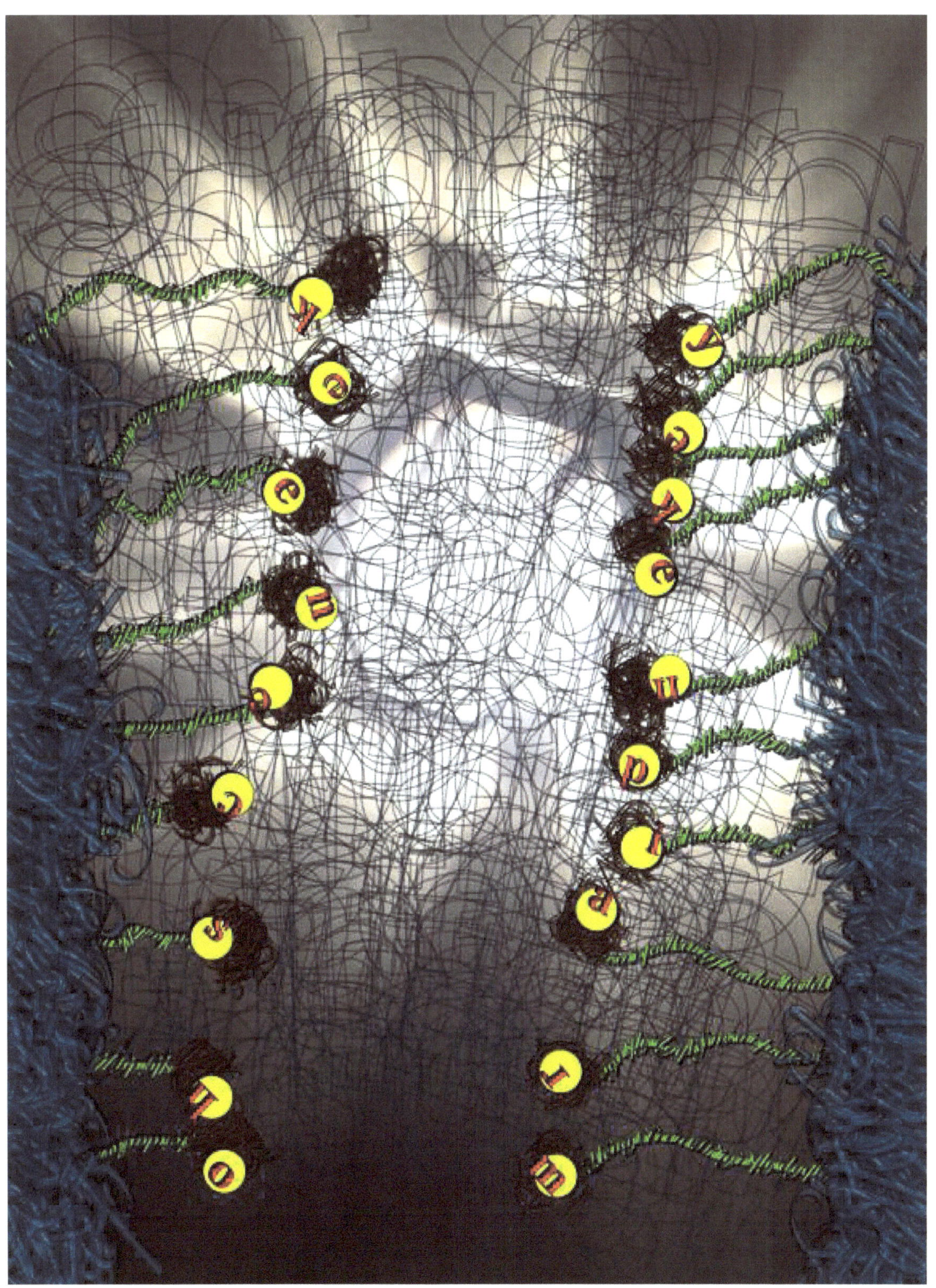

MAPS

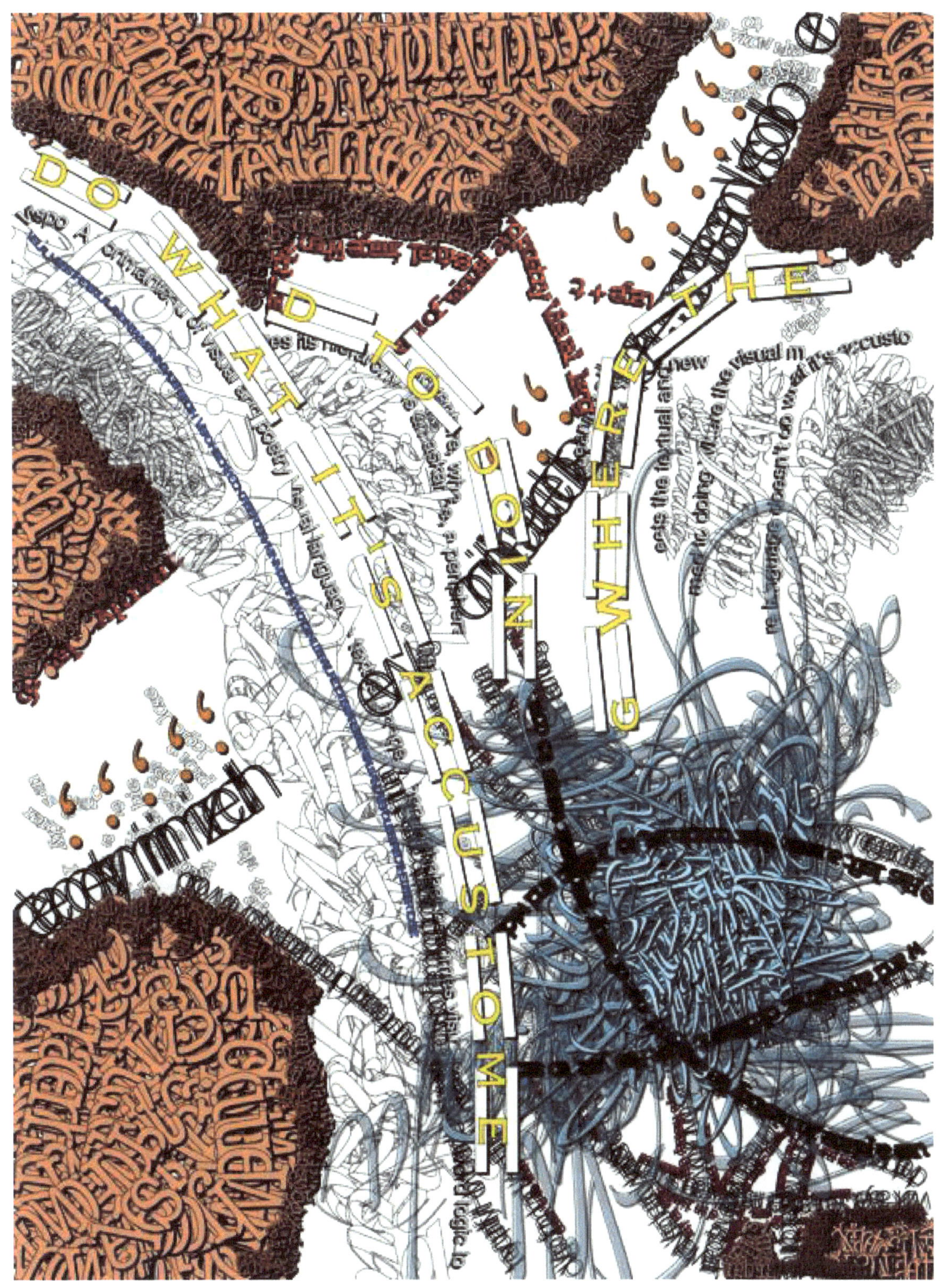

DO WHAT TO DO
WHAT IT'S ACCUSTOME
DOIN
WHERE THE
GOIN

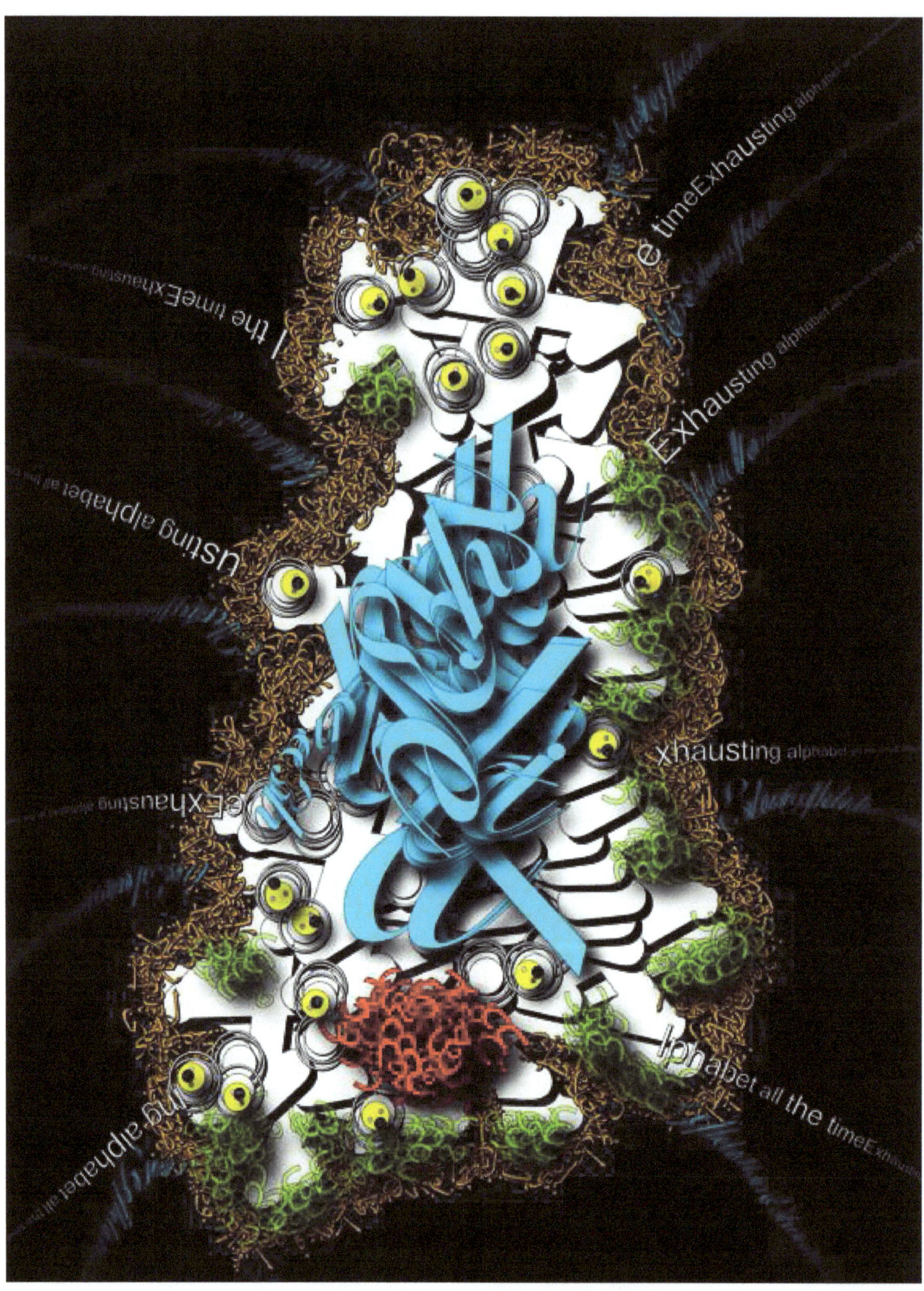

e timeExhausting alphabet
I the timeExhausting alphabet
usting alphabet
Exhausting alphabet
eExhausting alphabet
xhausting alphabet
lphabet all the timeExhausting
ing alphabet all the

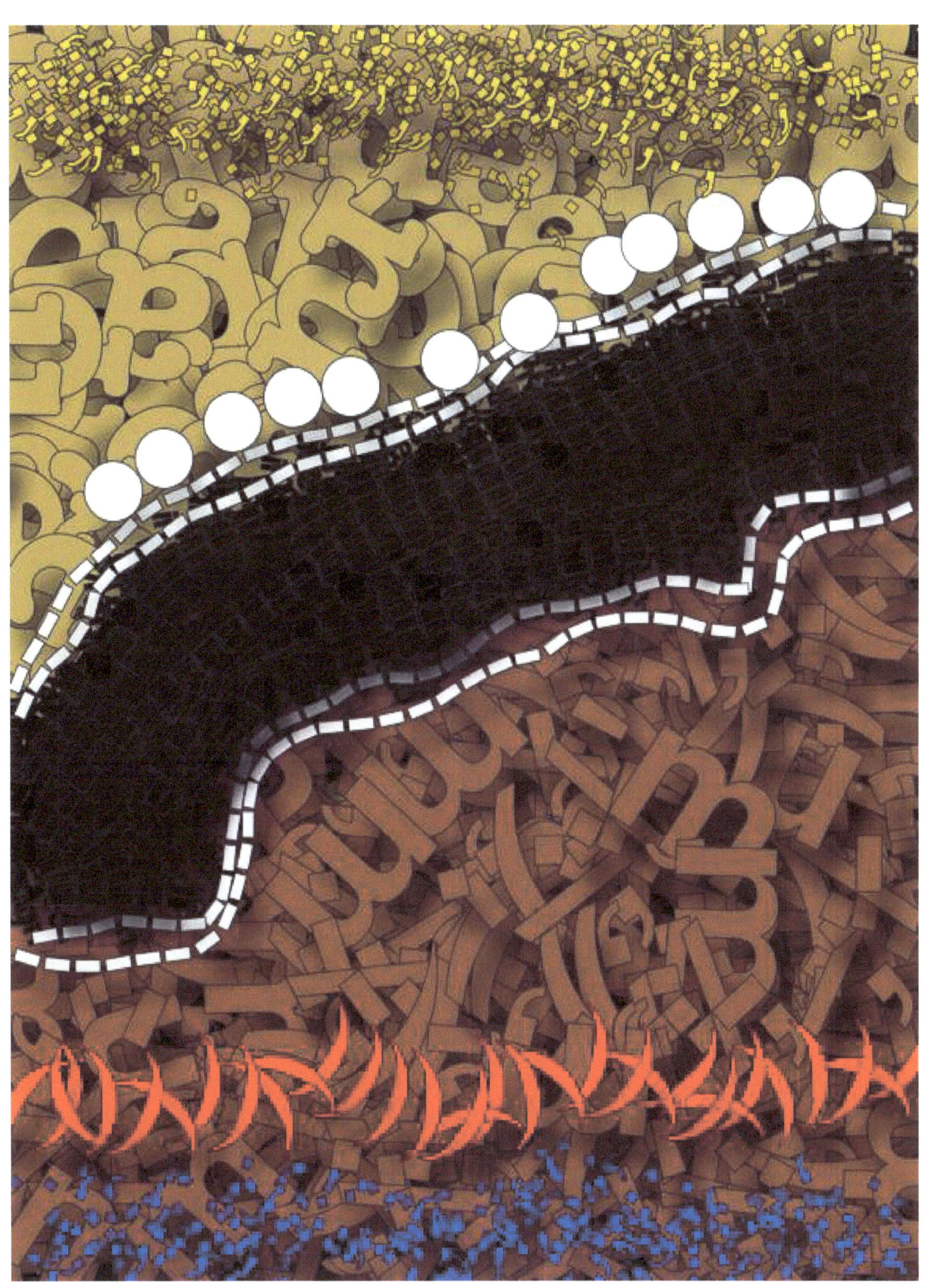

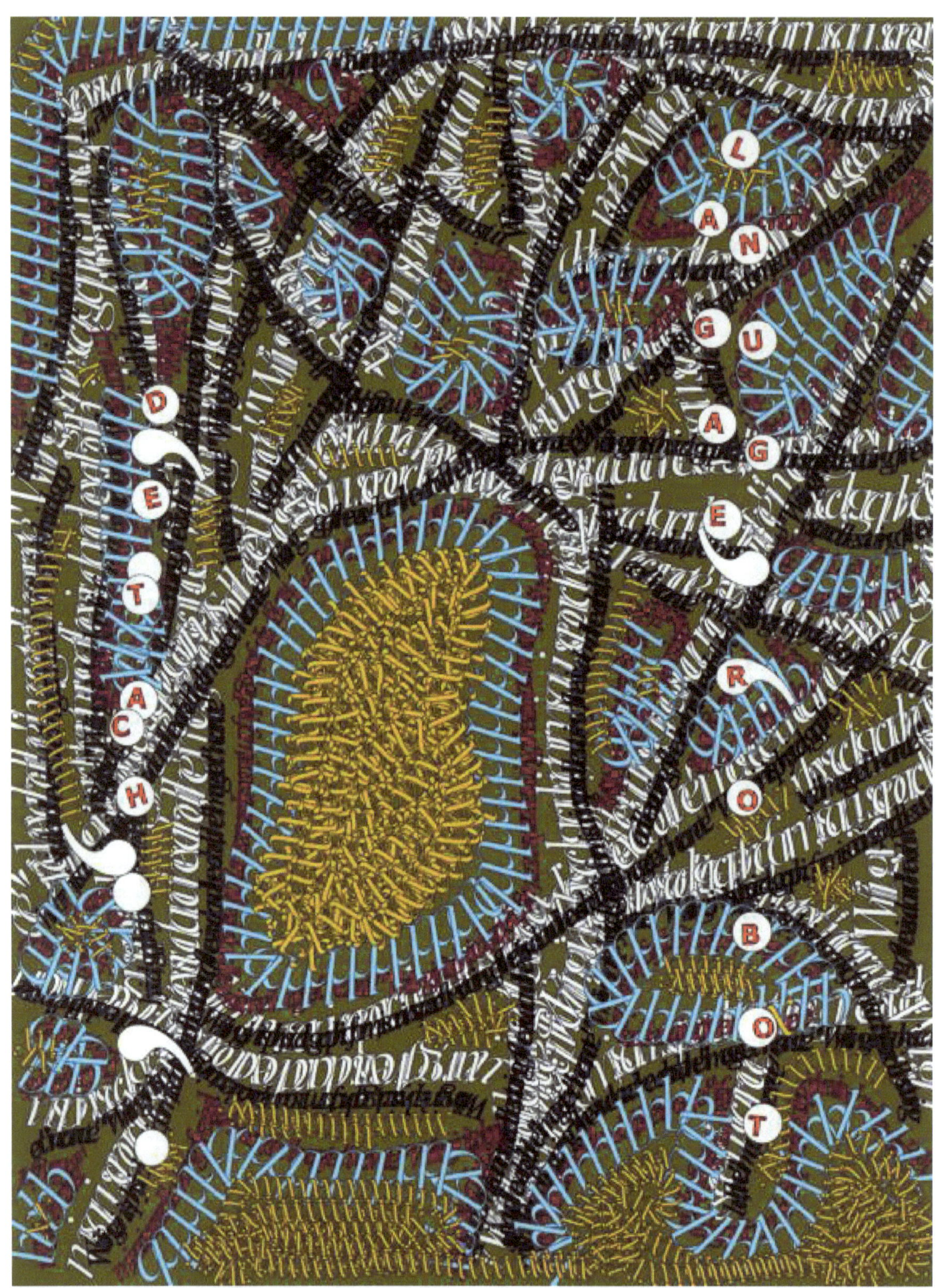

DETACH
LANGUAGE
ERROR
BOOT

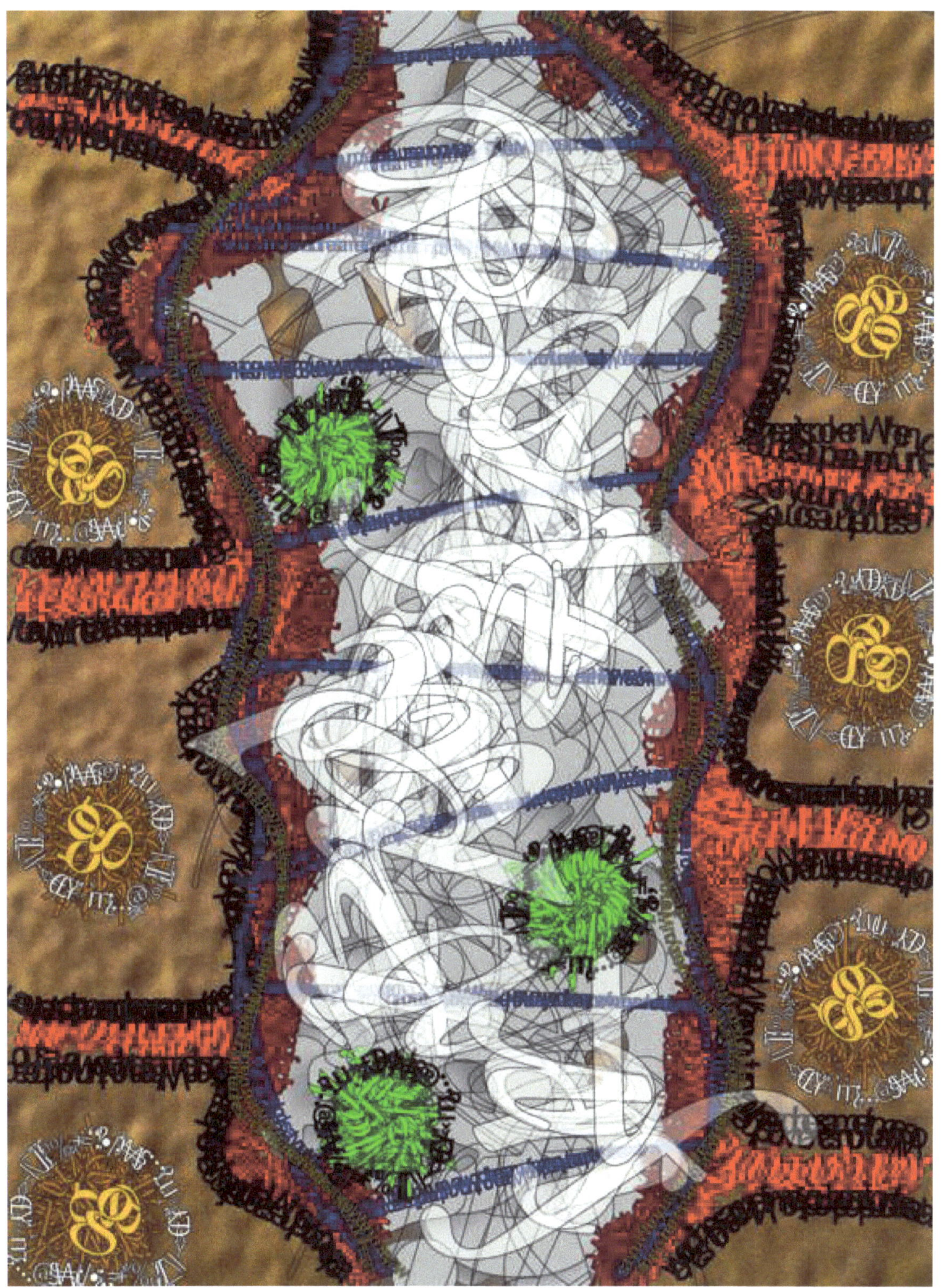

WAYS TO BEGIN

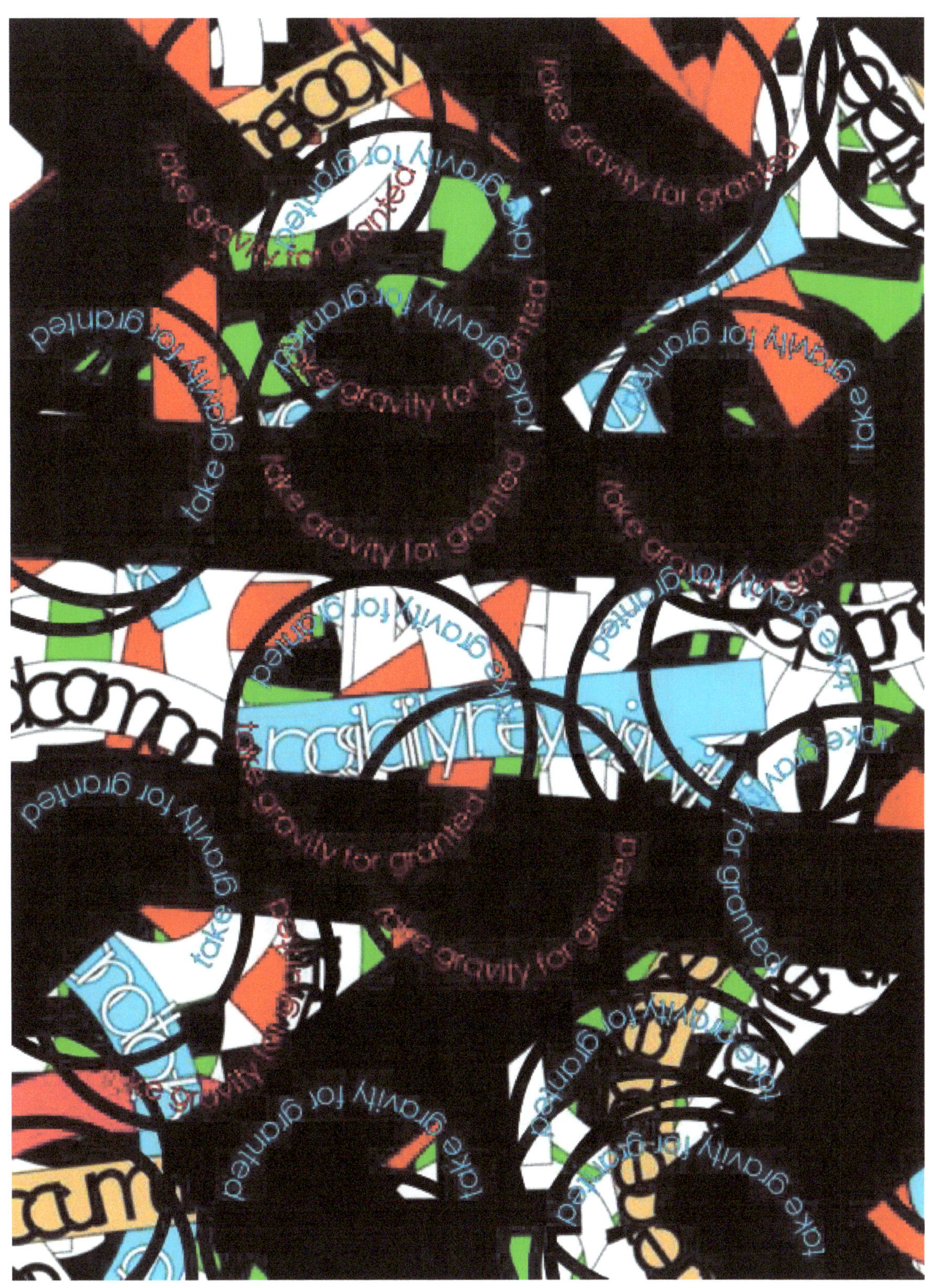

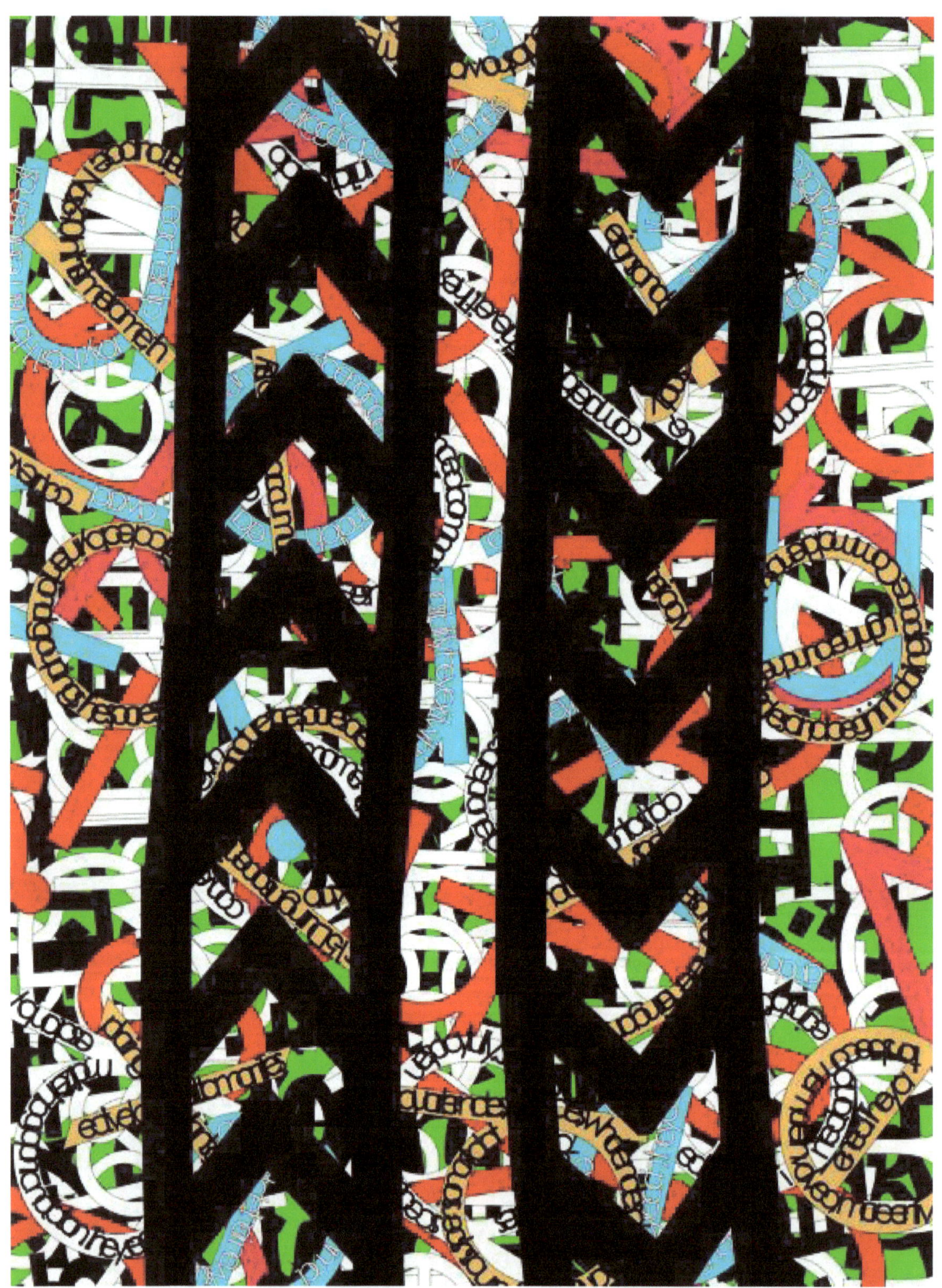

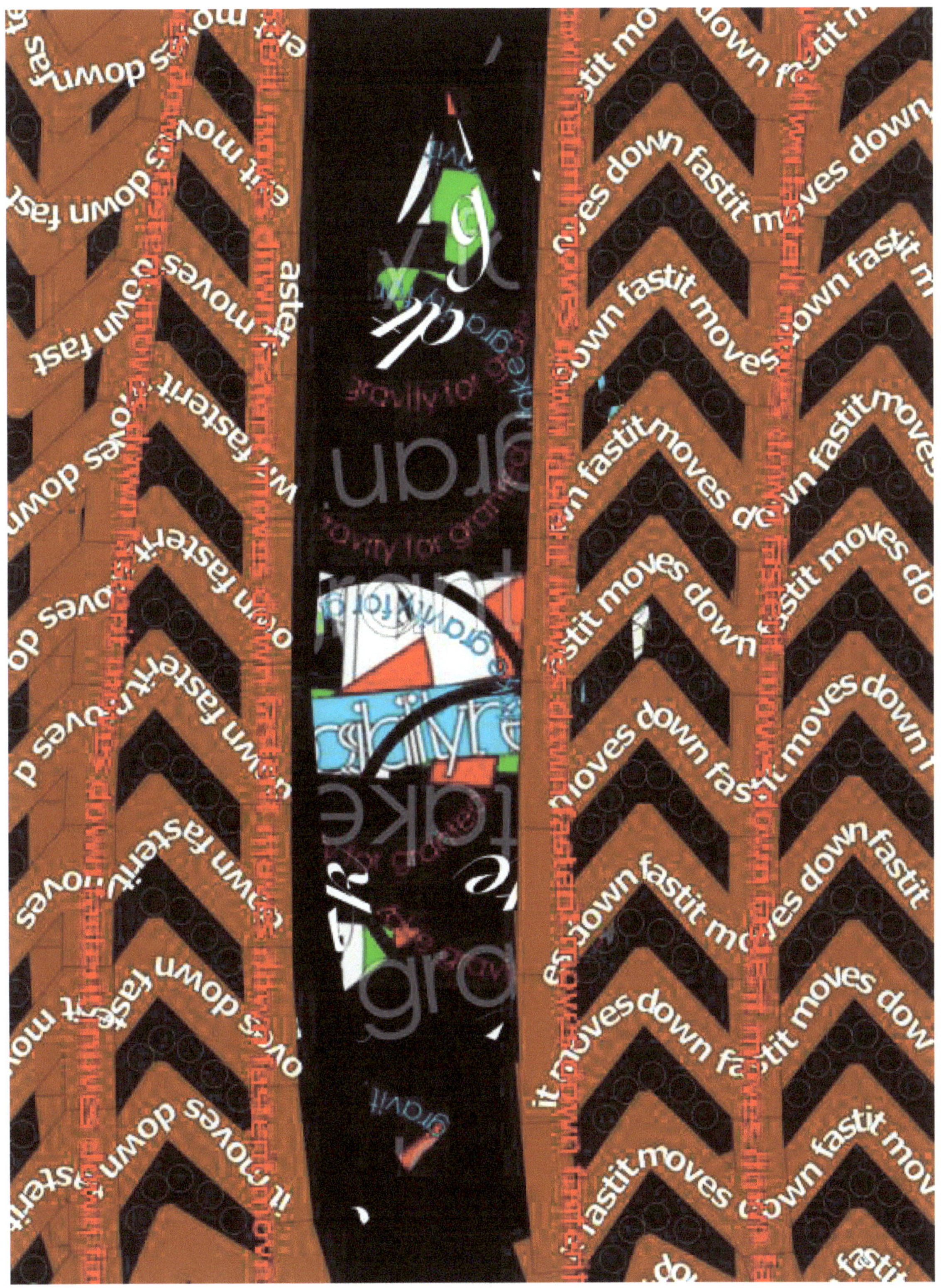
it moves down fast
gravity
grab
take

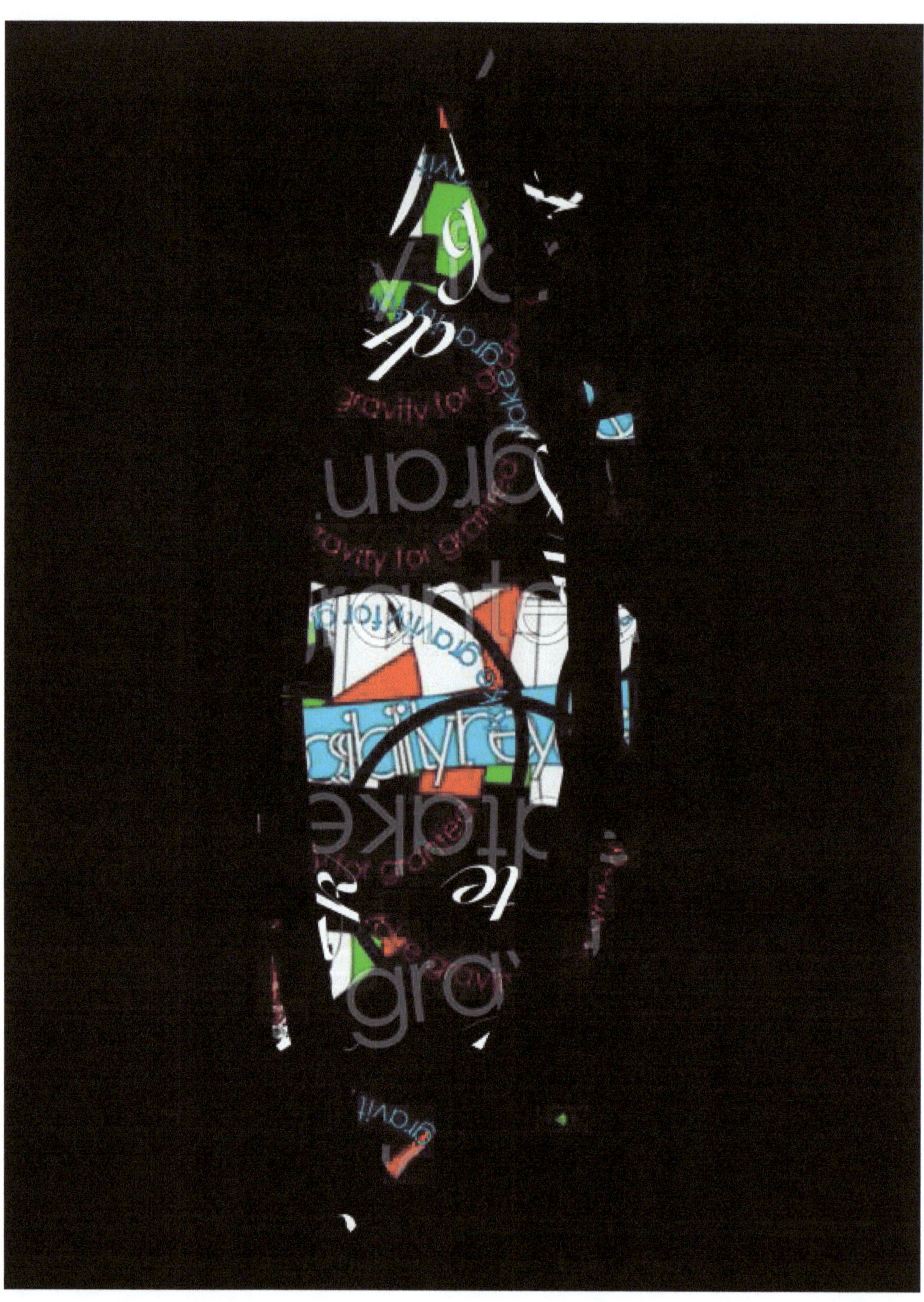

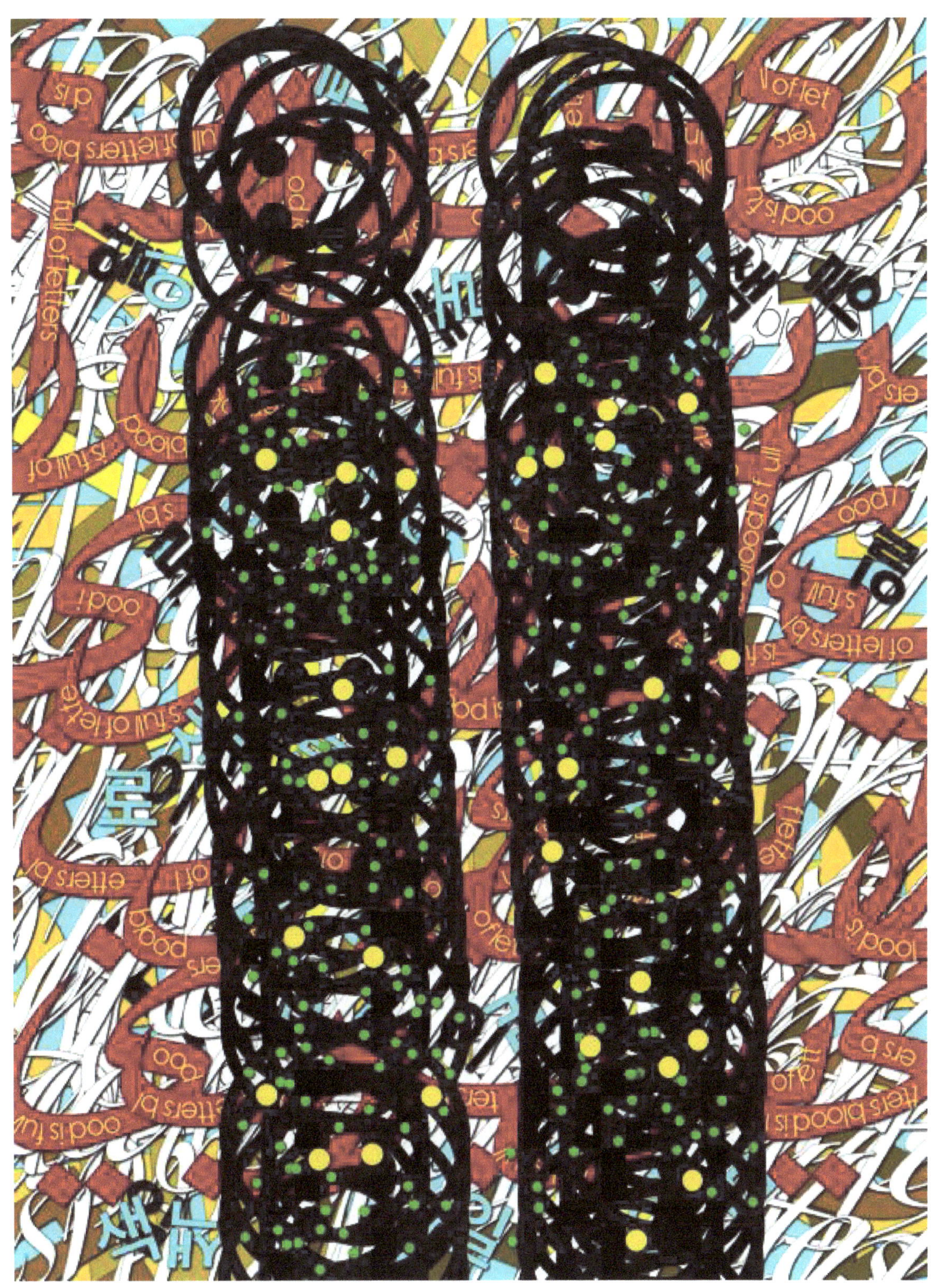

CLOSE
TO
OVER

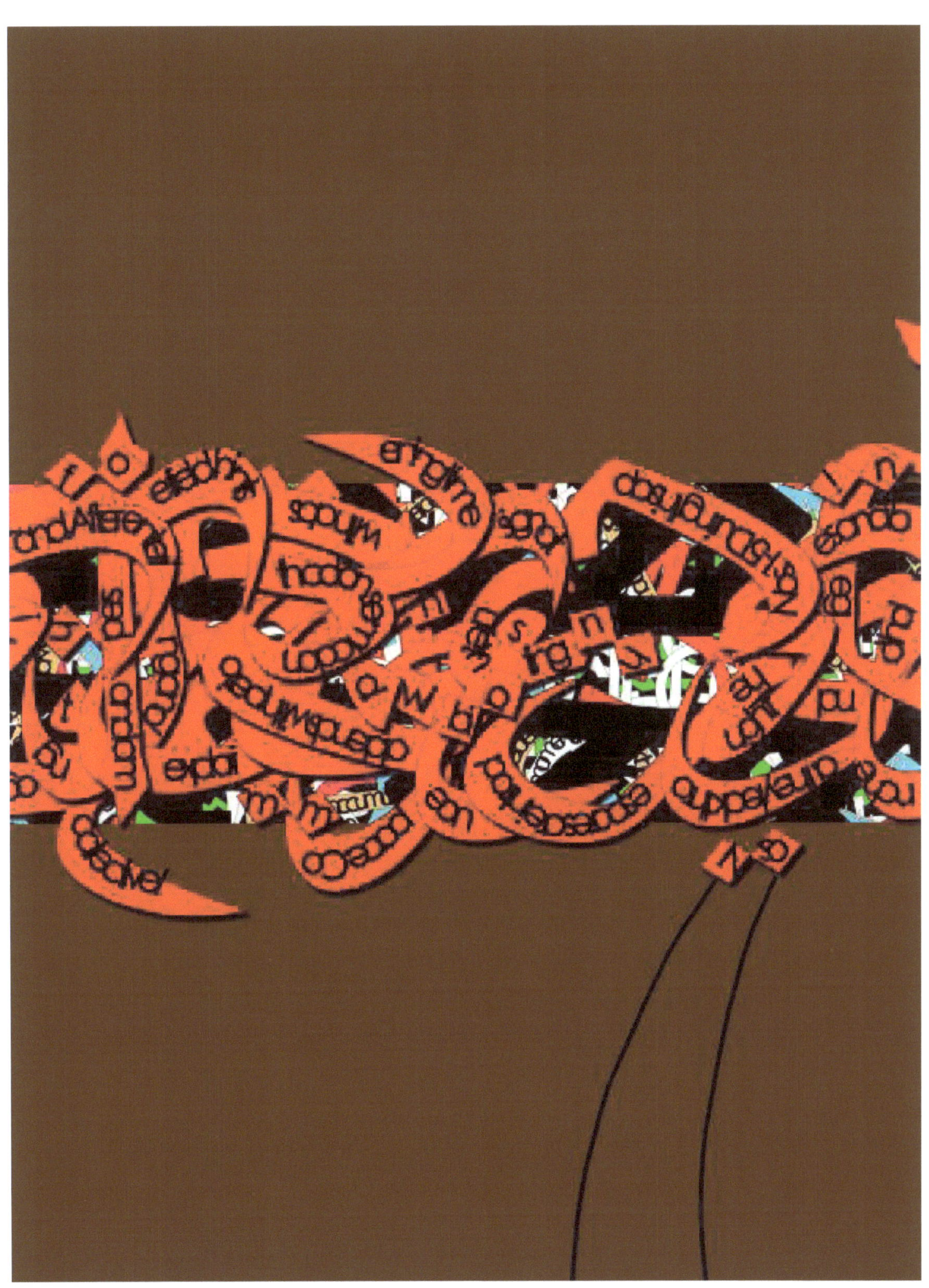

BEADS

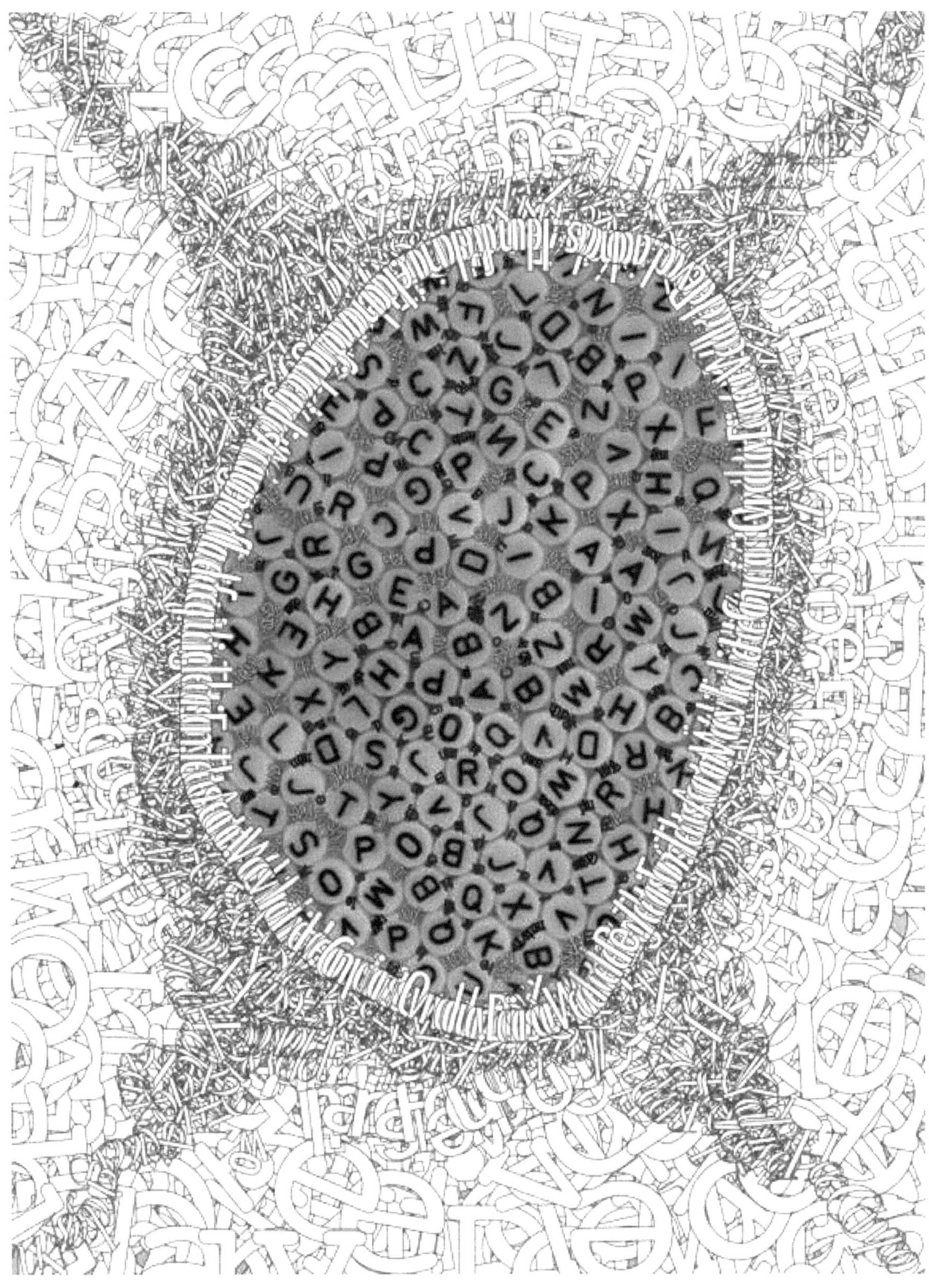

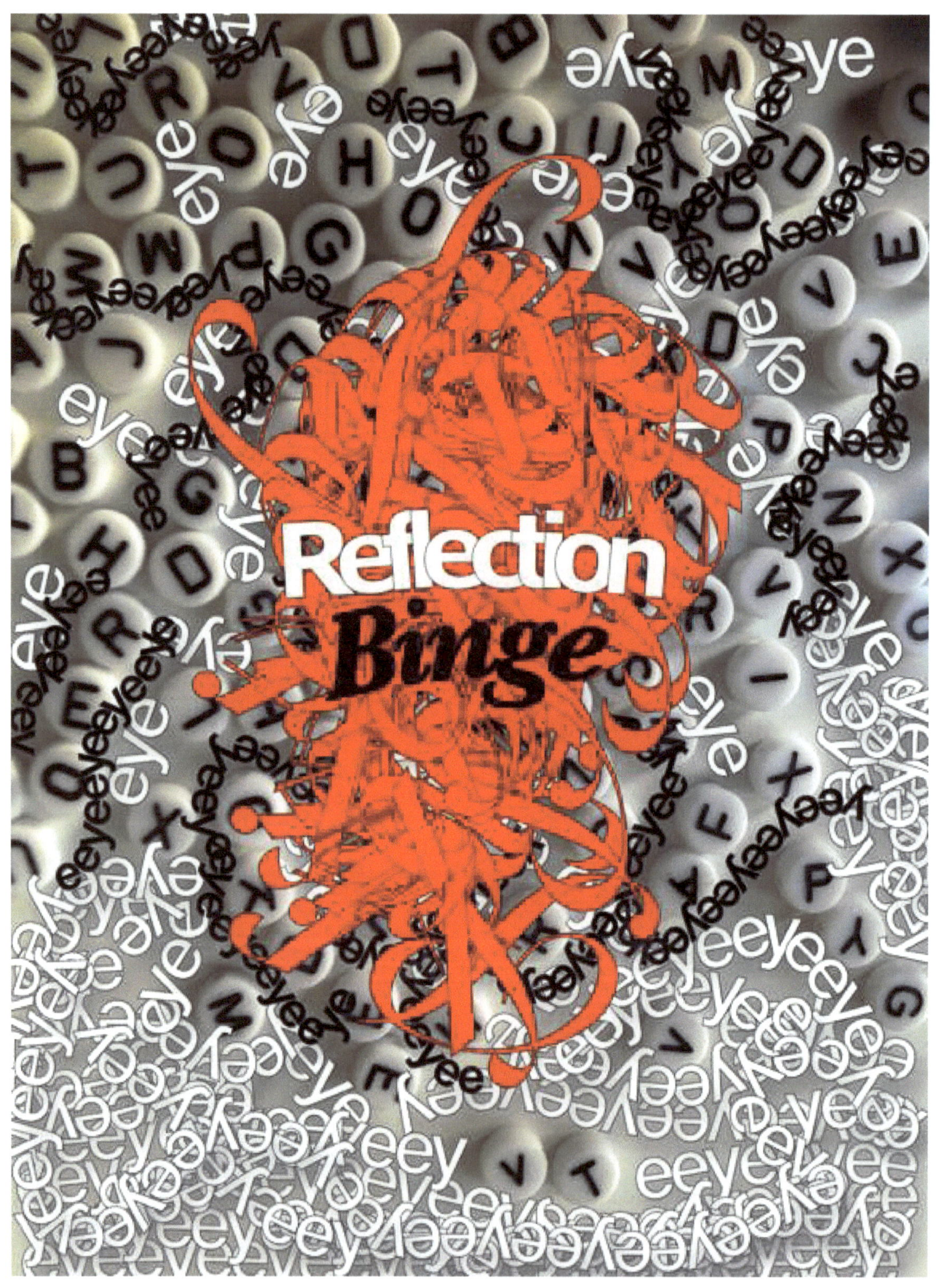
Reflection
Binge

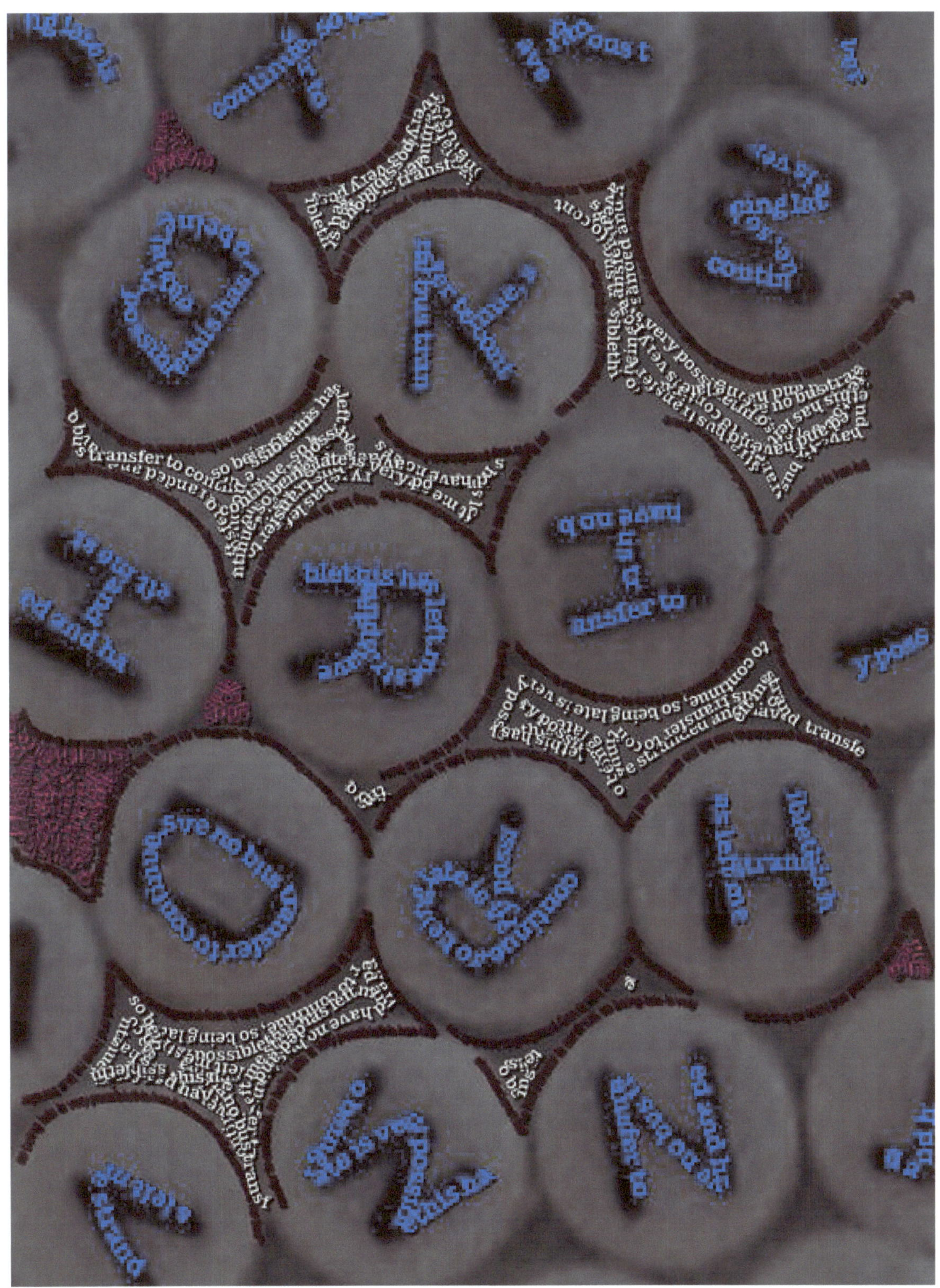

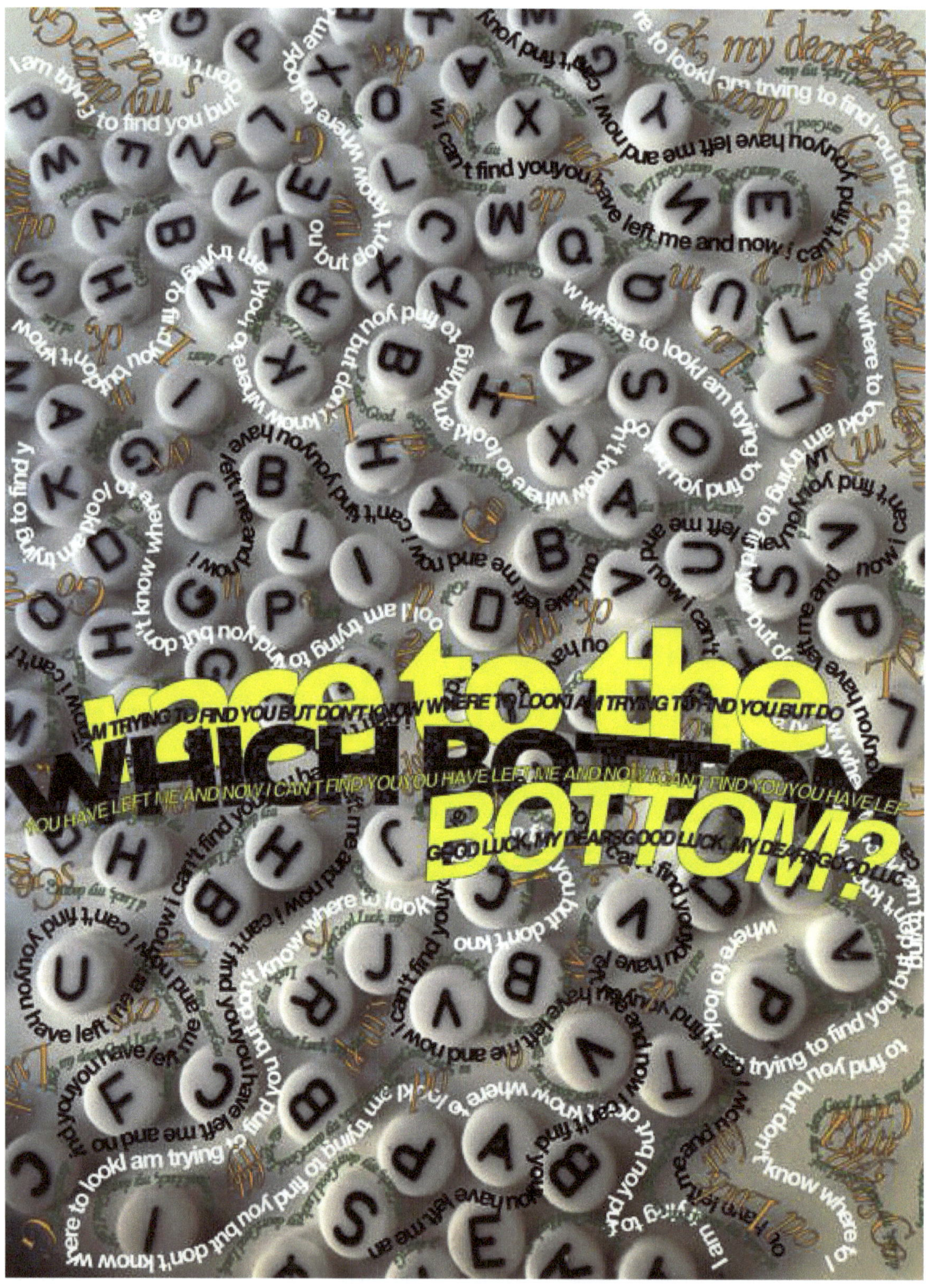
race to the
WHICH BOTTOM
BOTTOM?

OPPOSITES

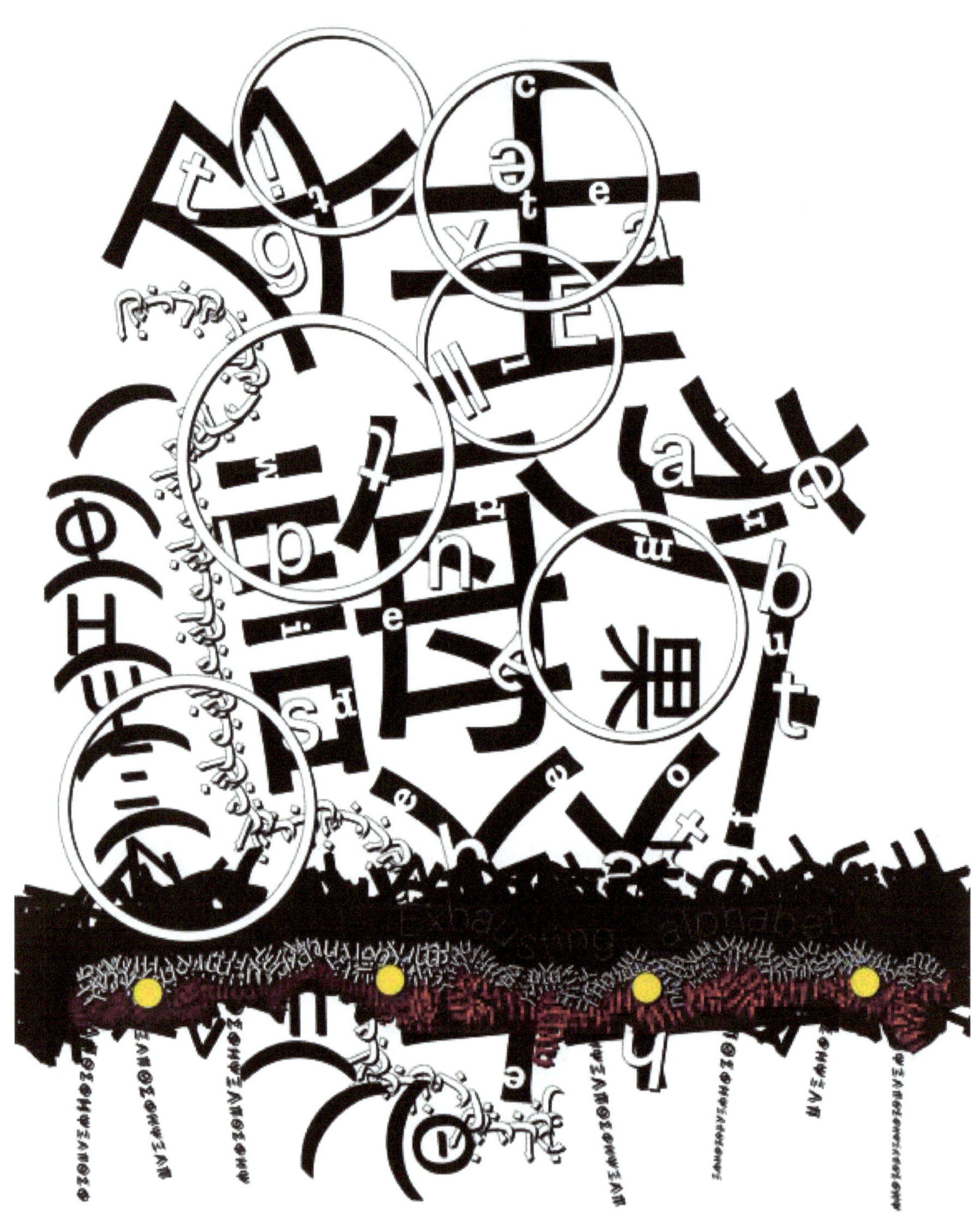

Exhausting alphabet

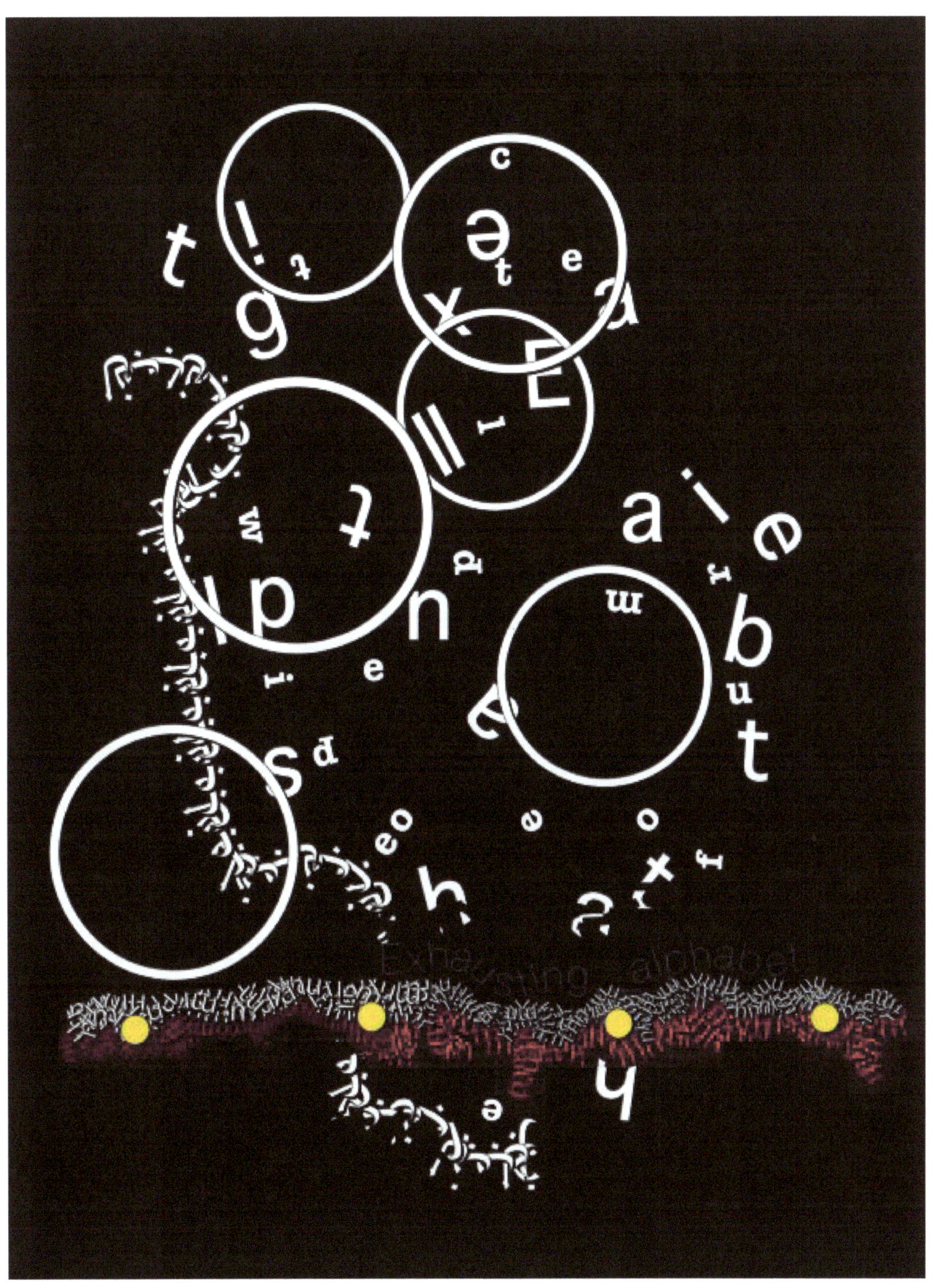
Exhausting alphabet

ANIMALS INSIDE WORDS

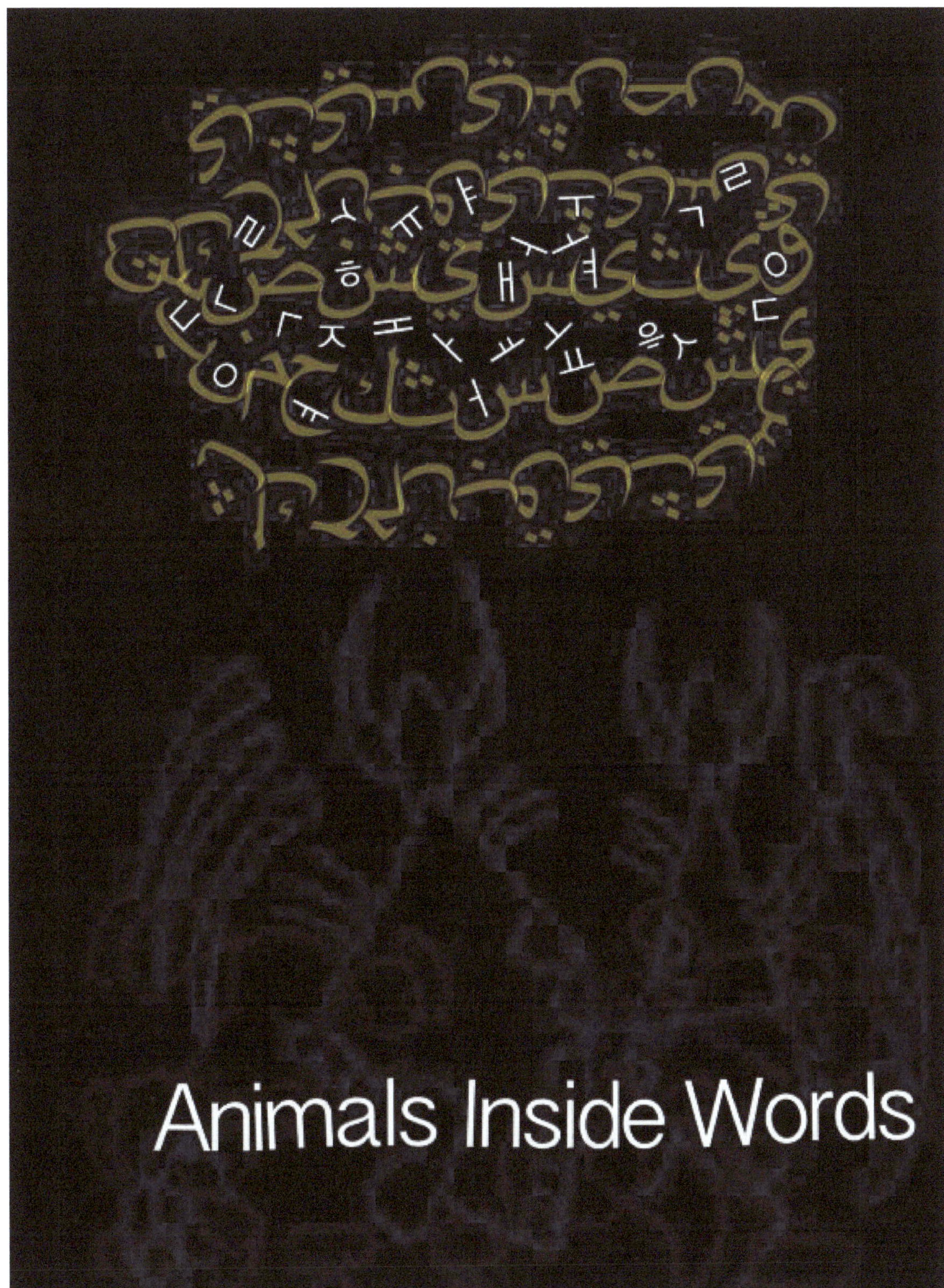

Animals Inside Words

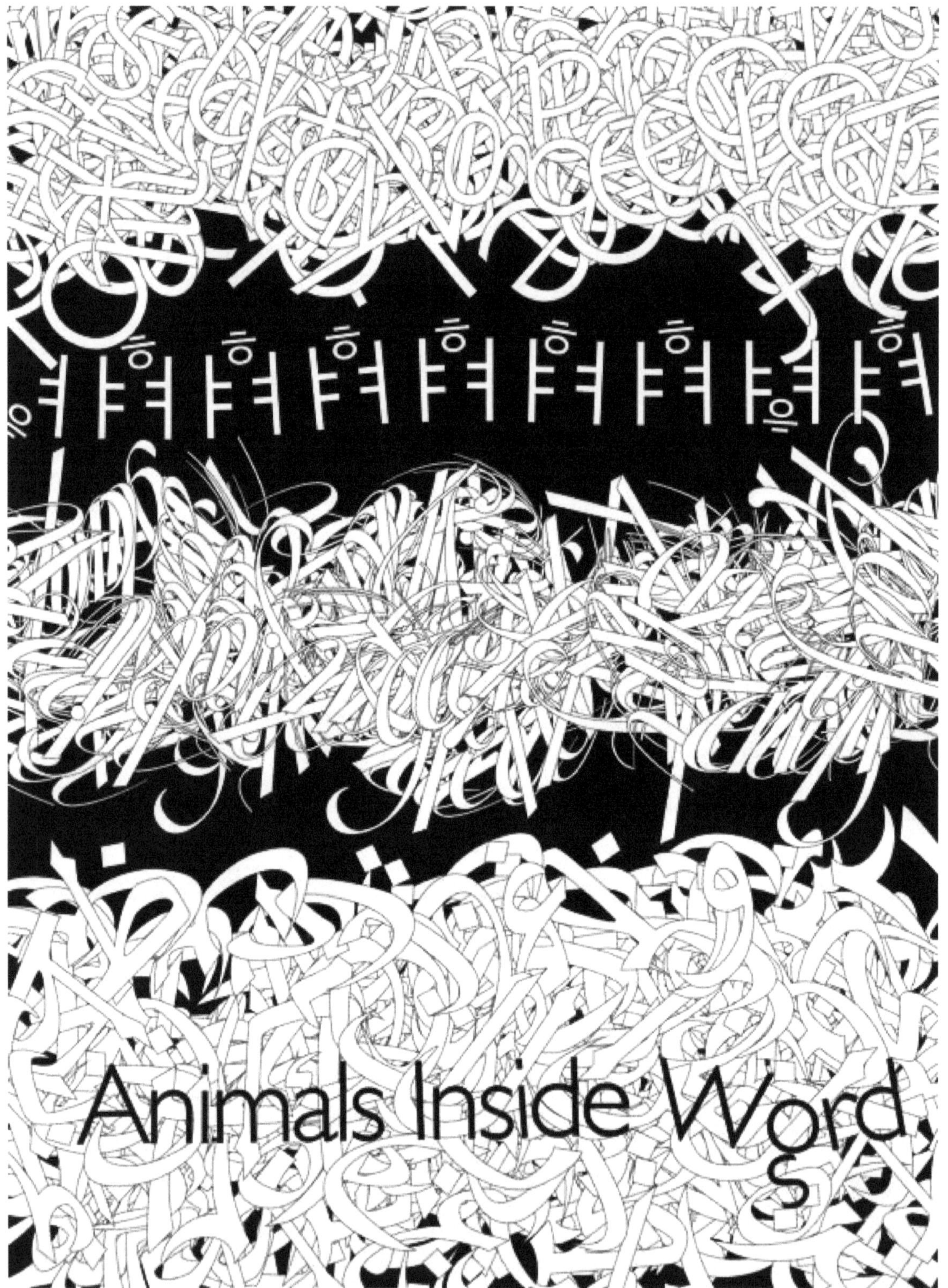

Animals Inside Words

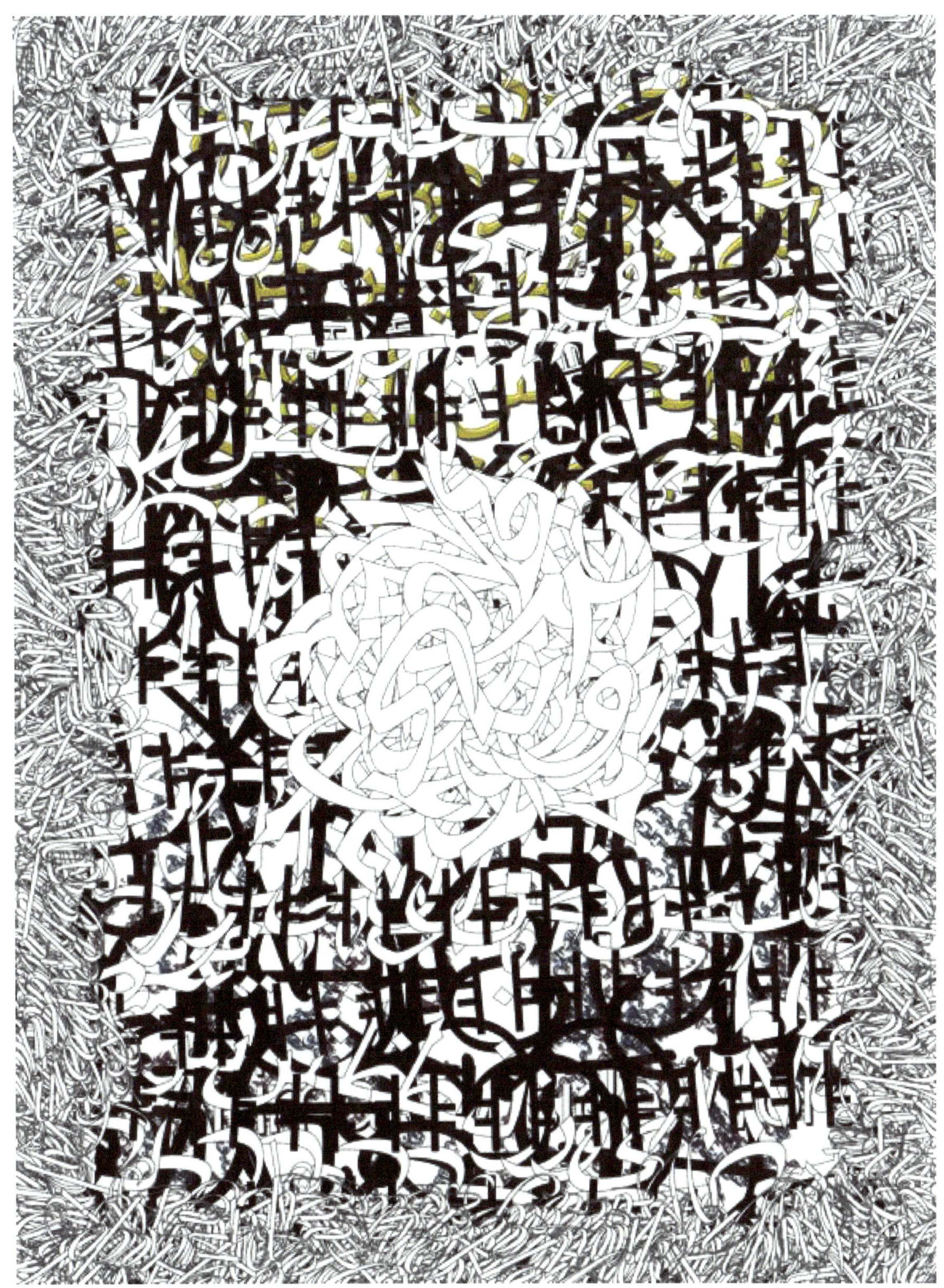

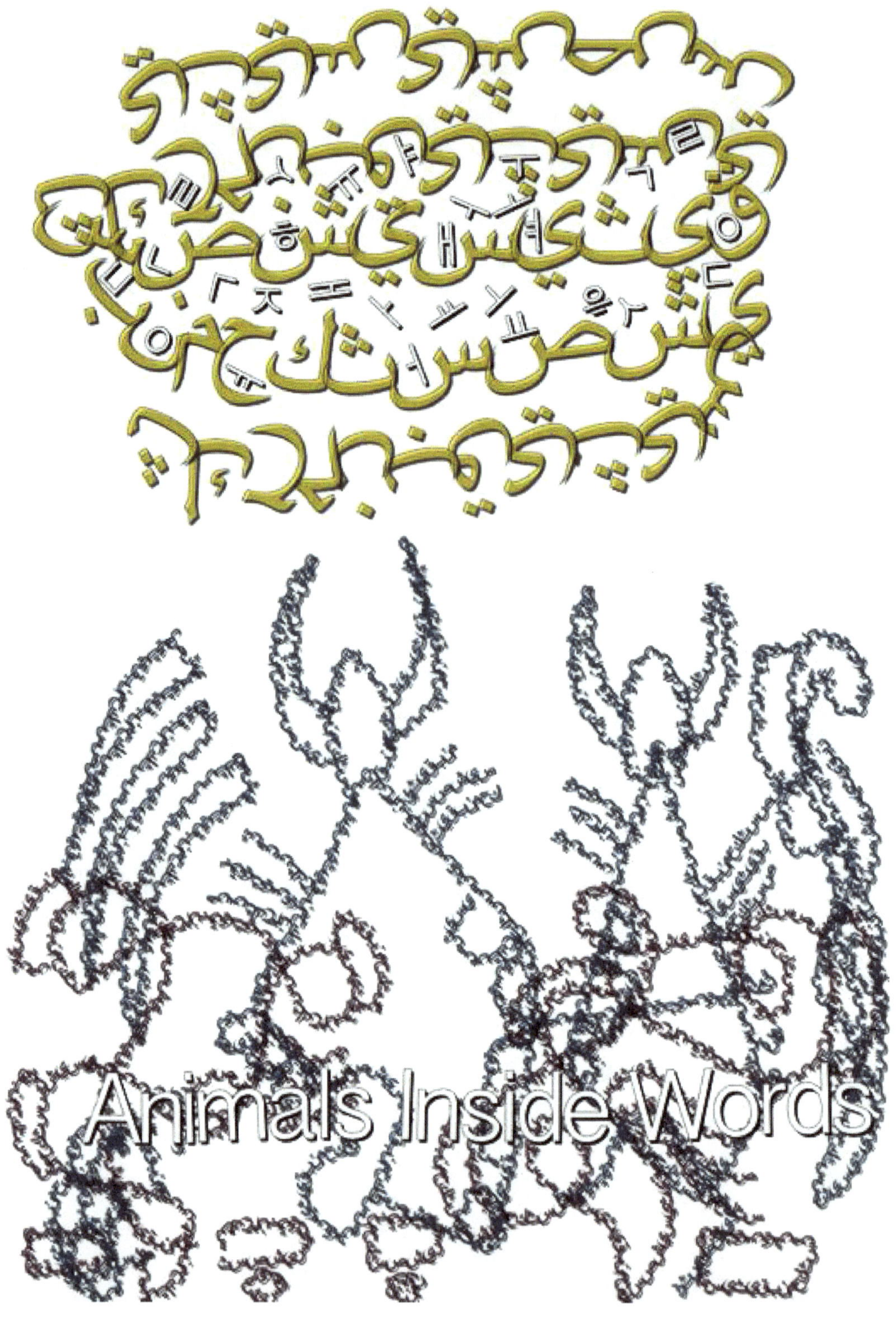
Animals Inside Words

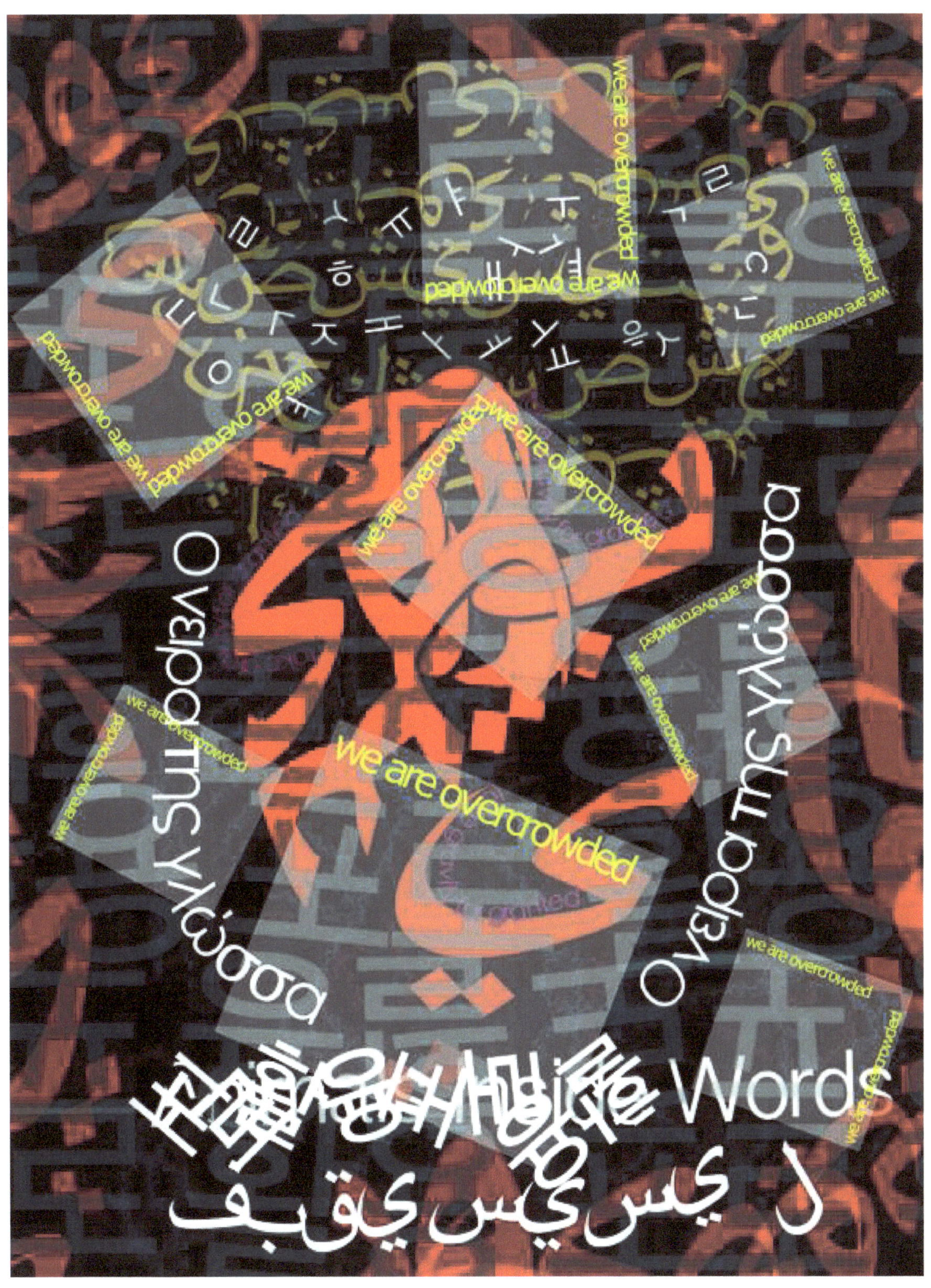

we are overcrowded
Overpopulating
Words

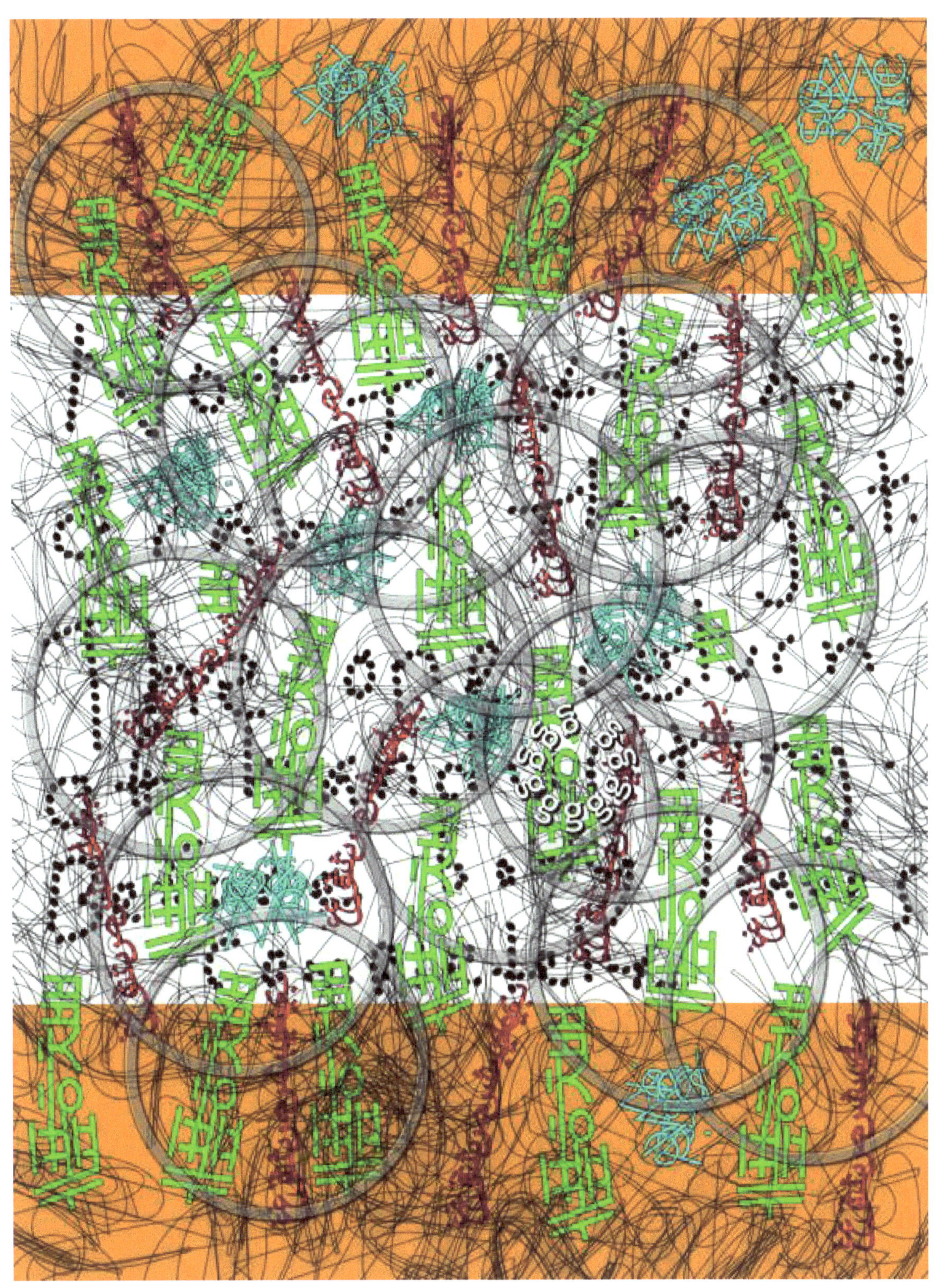

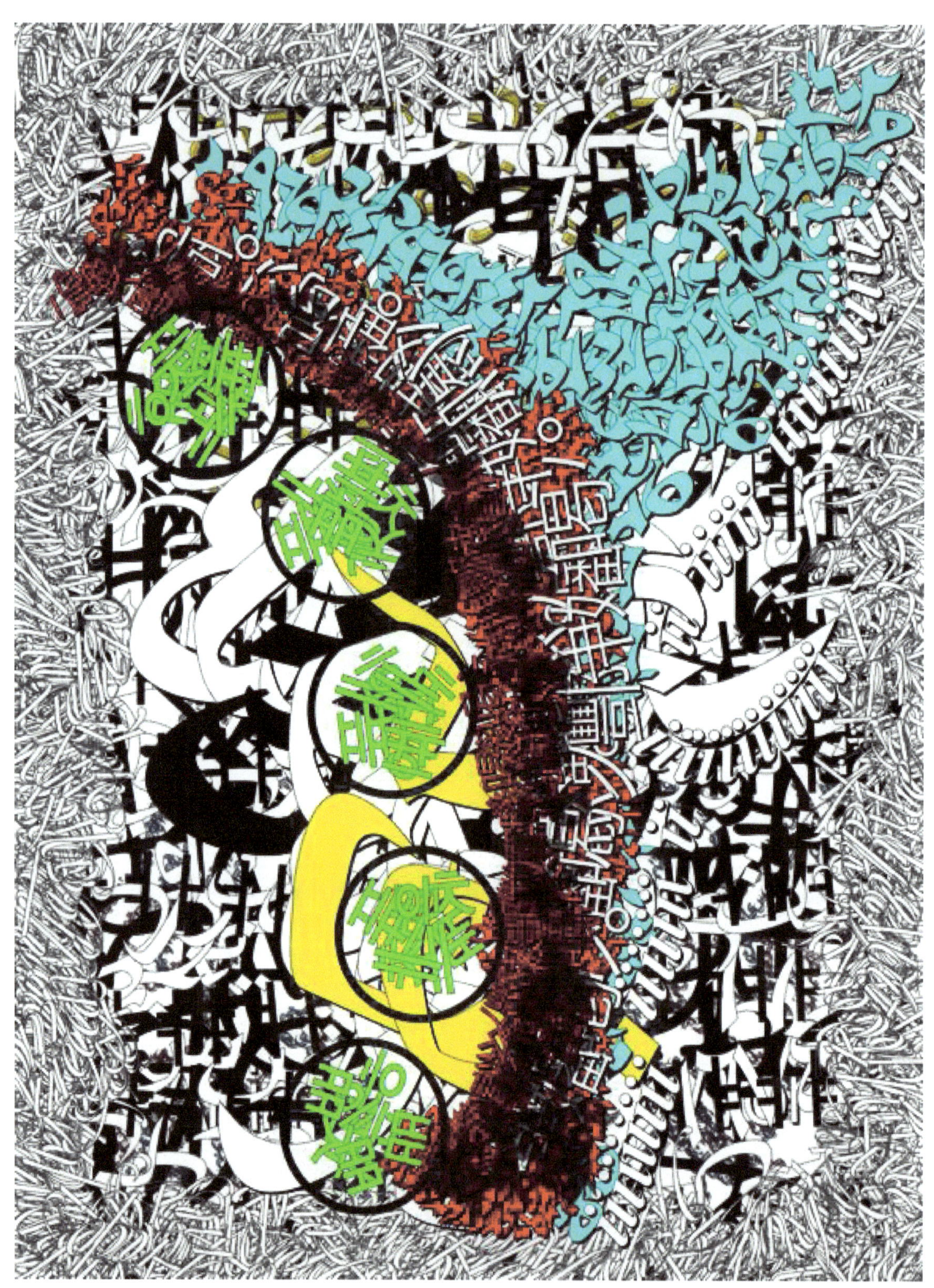

DOUBLES

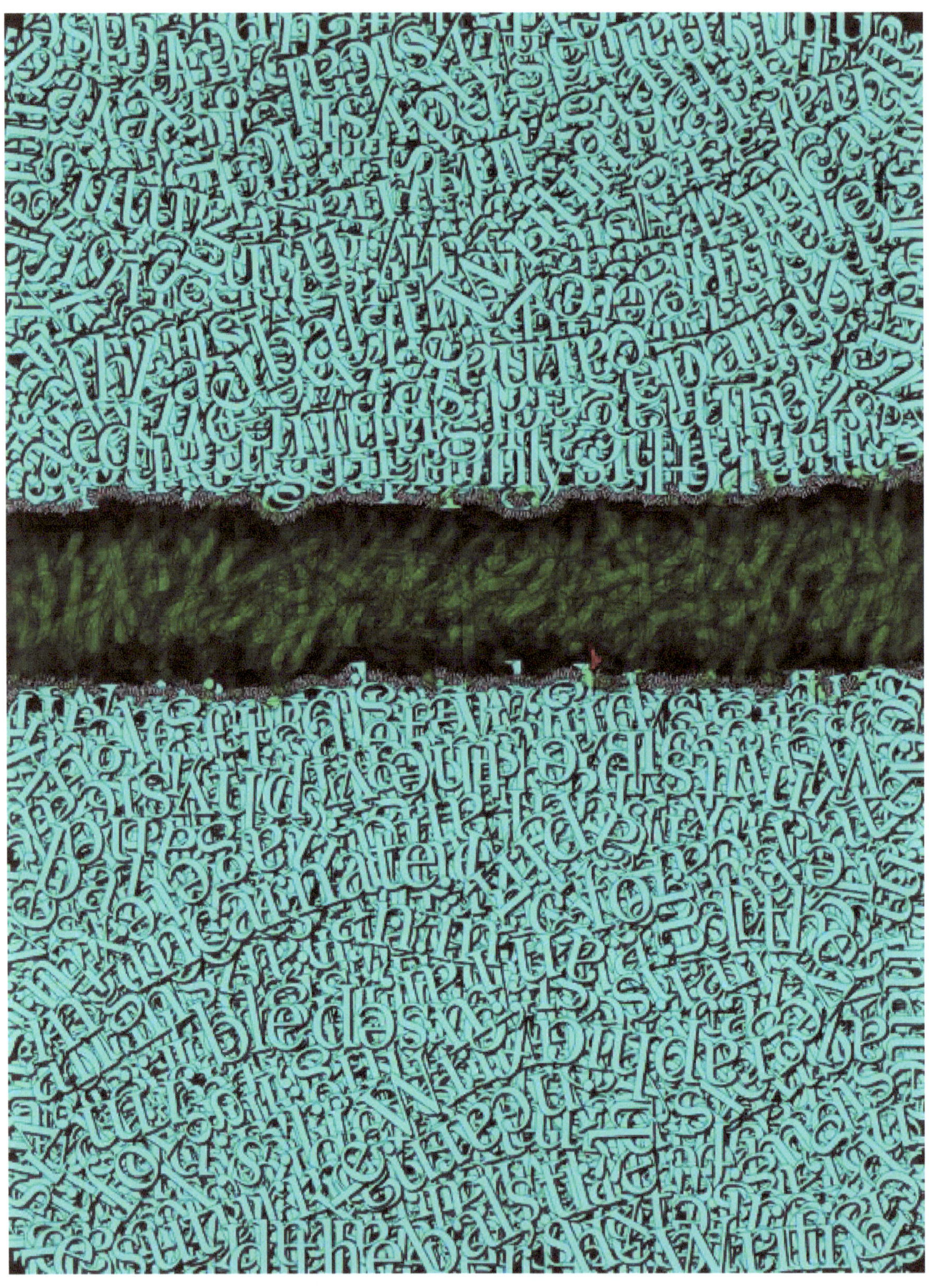

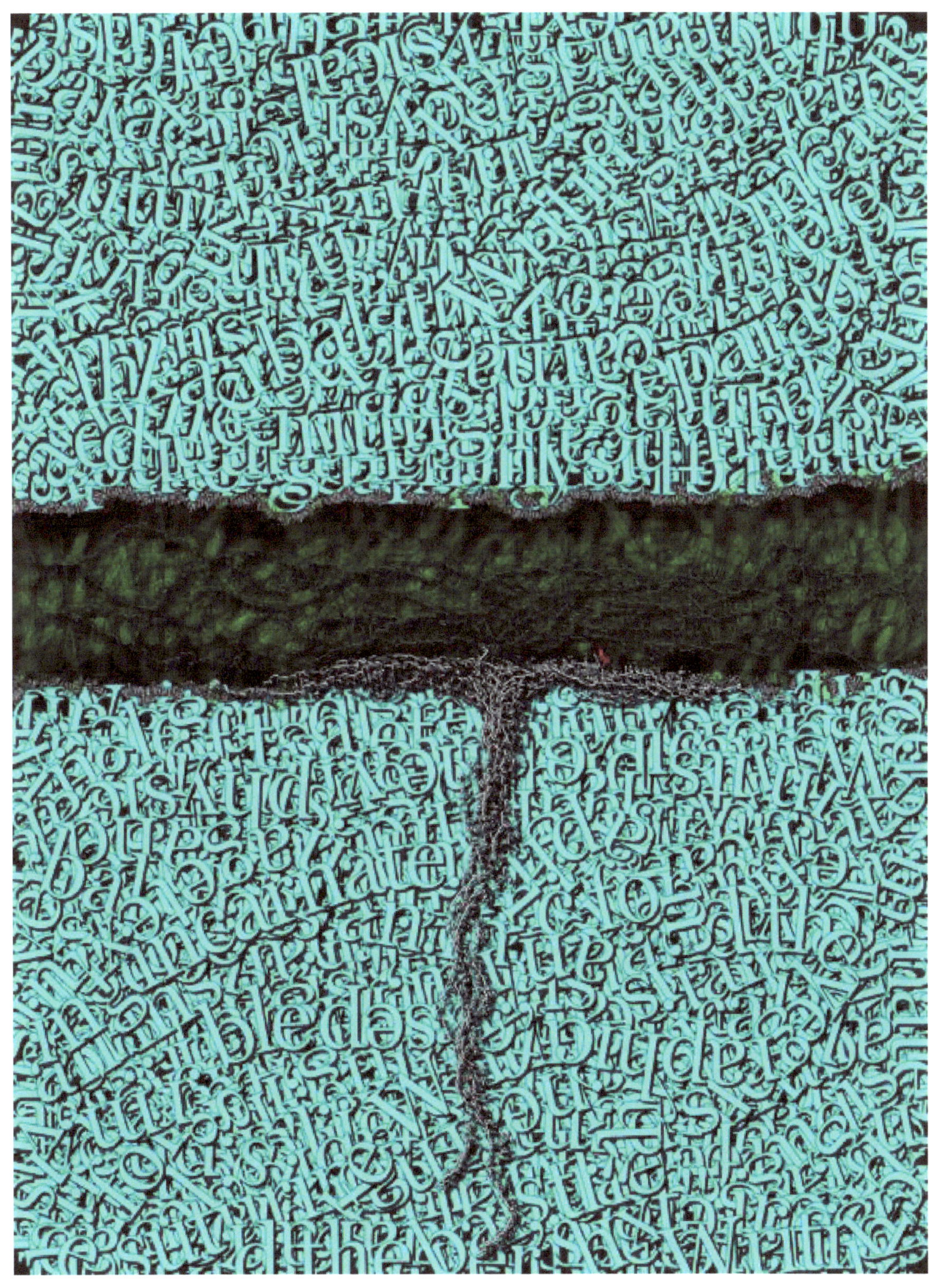

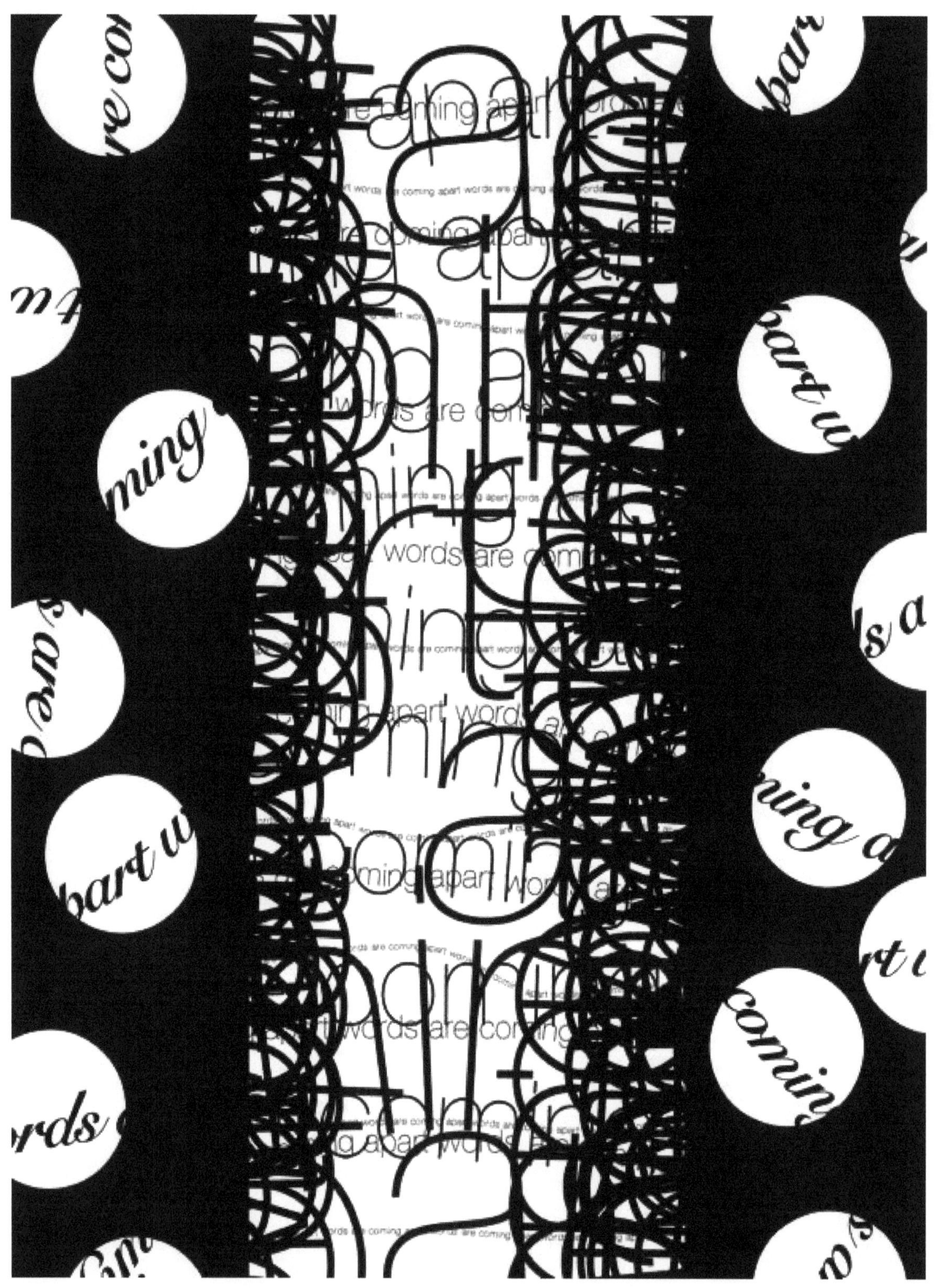

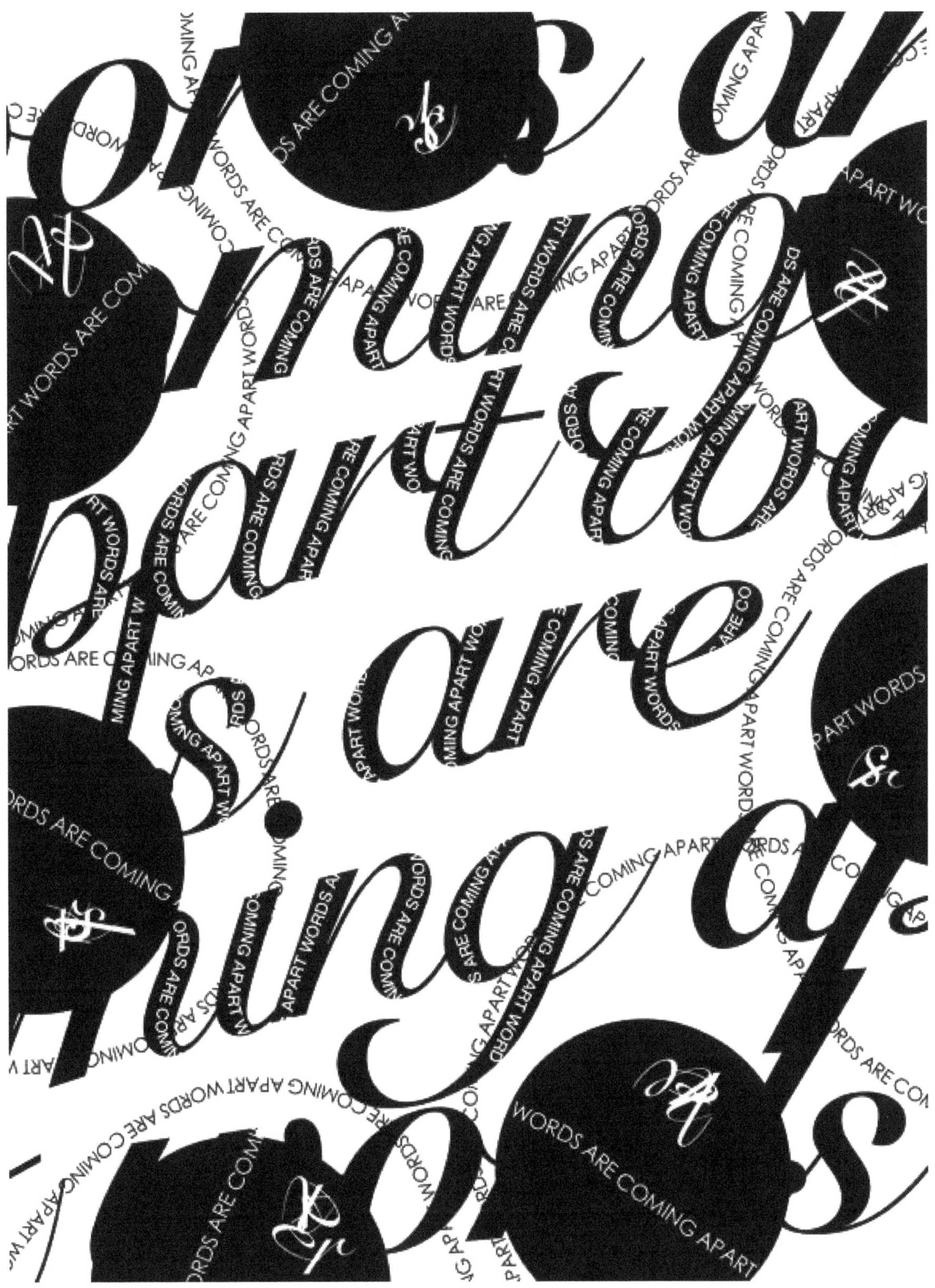

WORDS ARE COMING APART

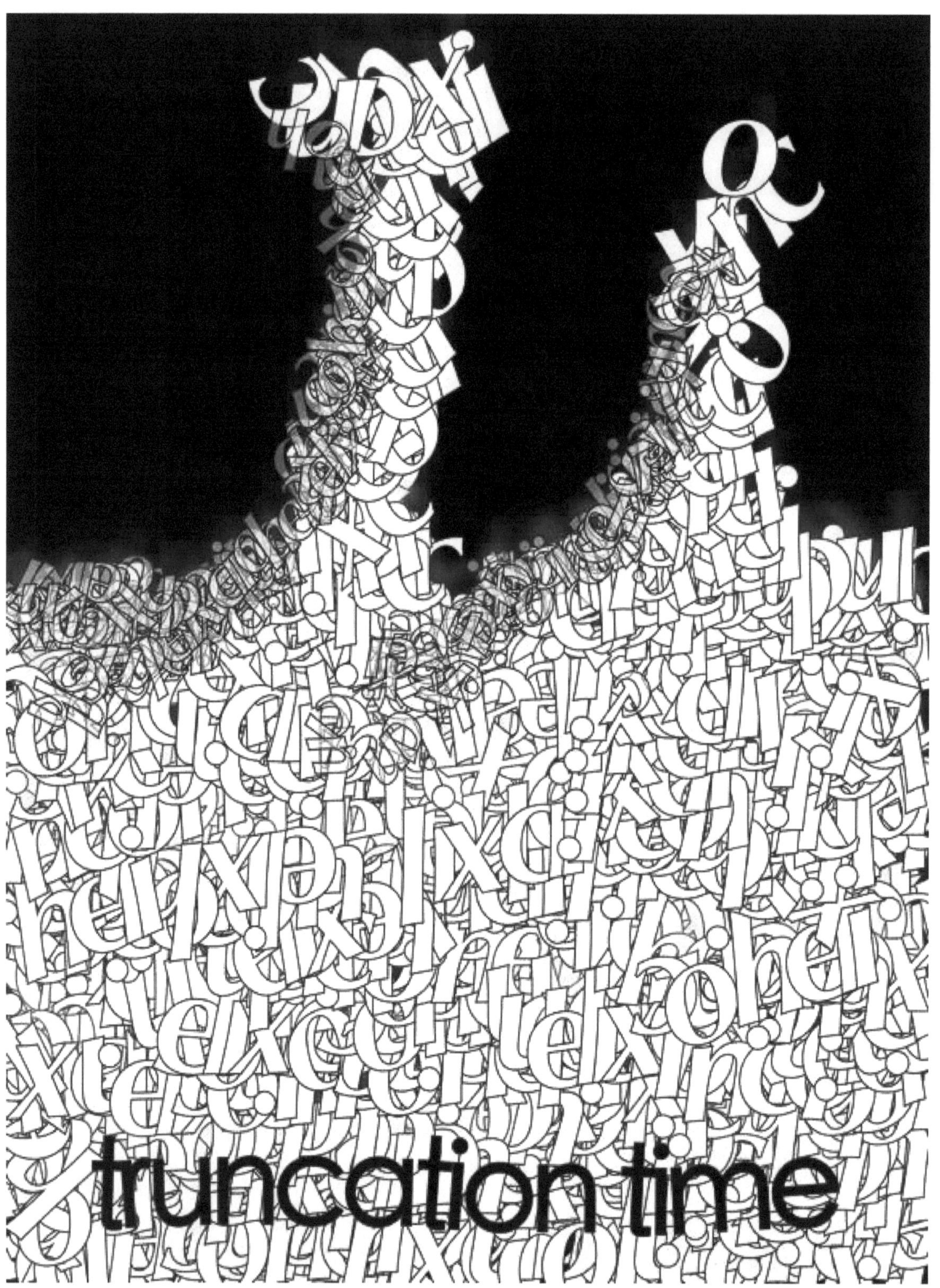

truncation time

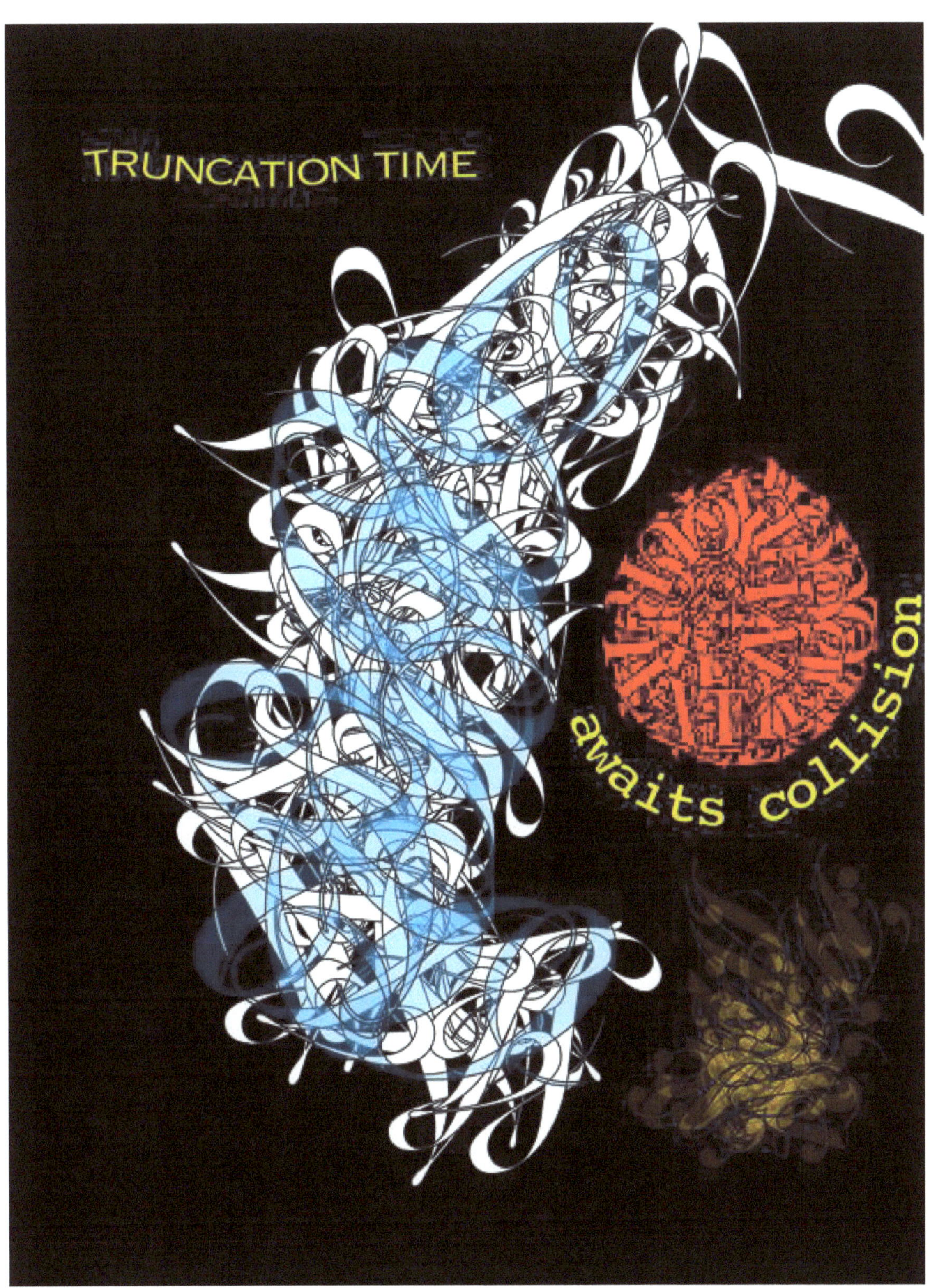
TRUNCATION TIME
awaits collision

FINERY

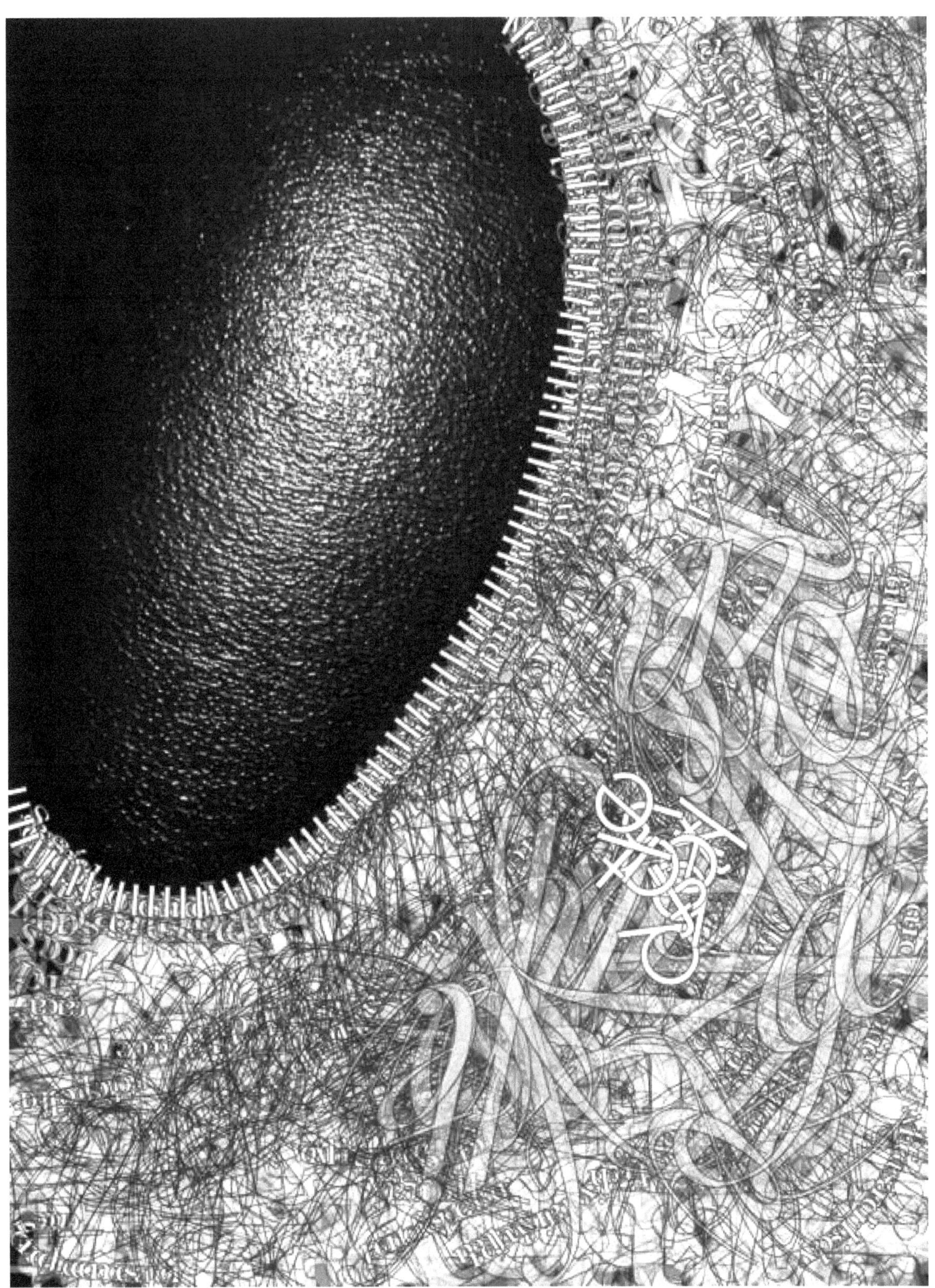

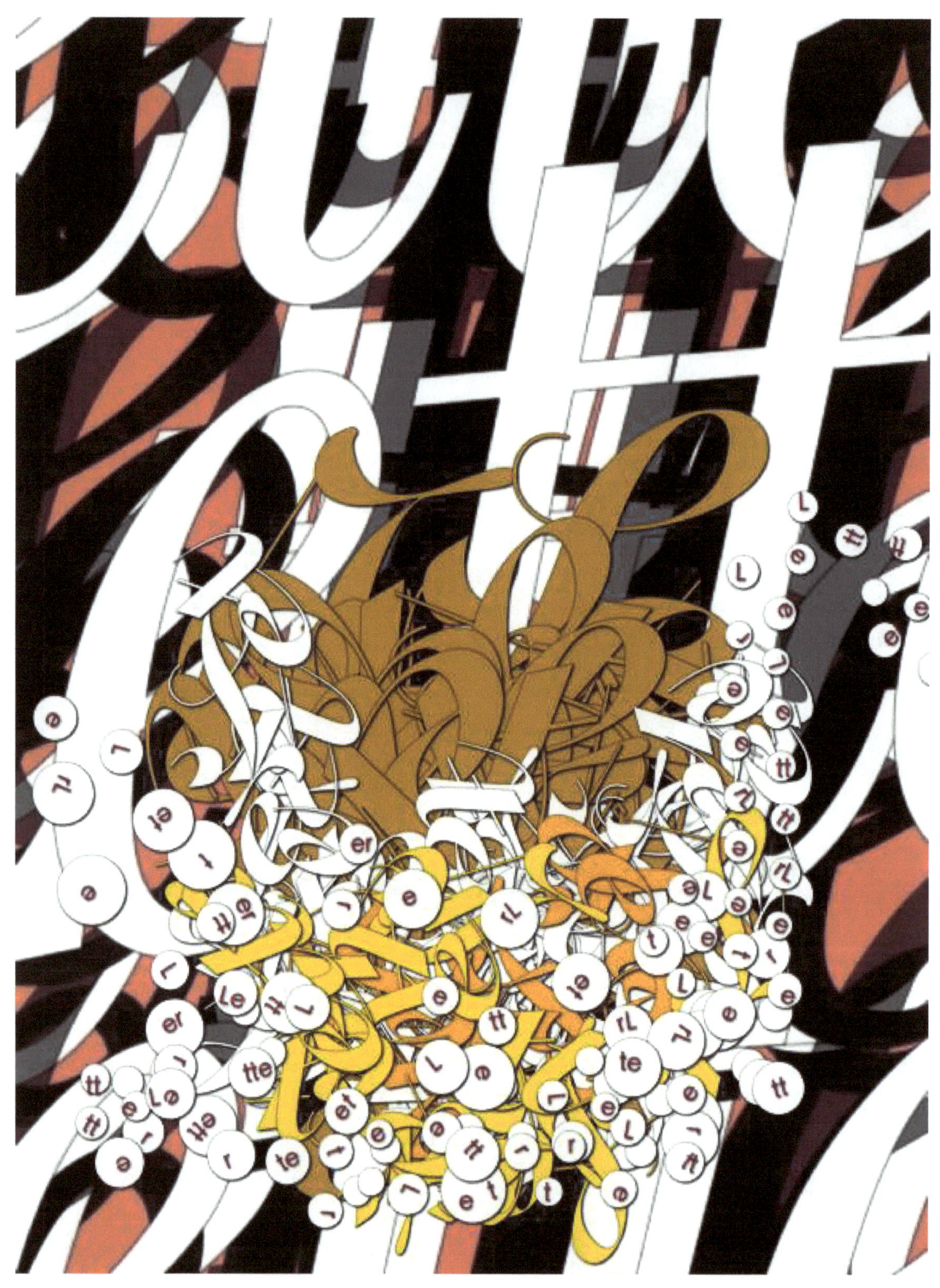

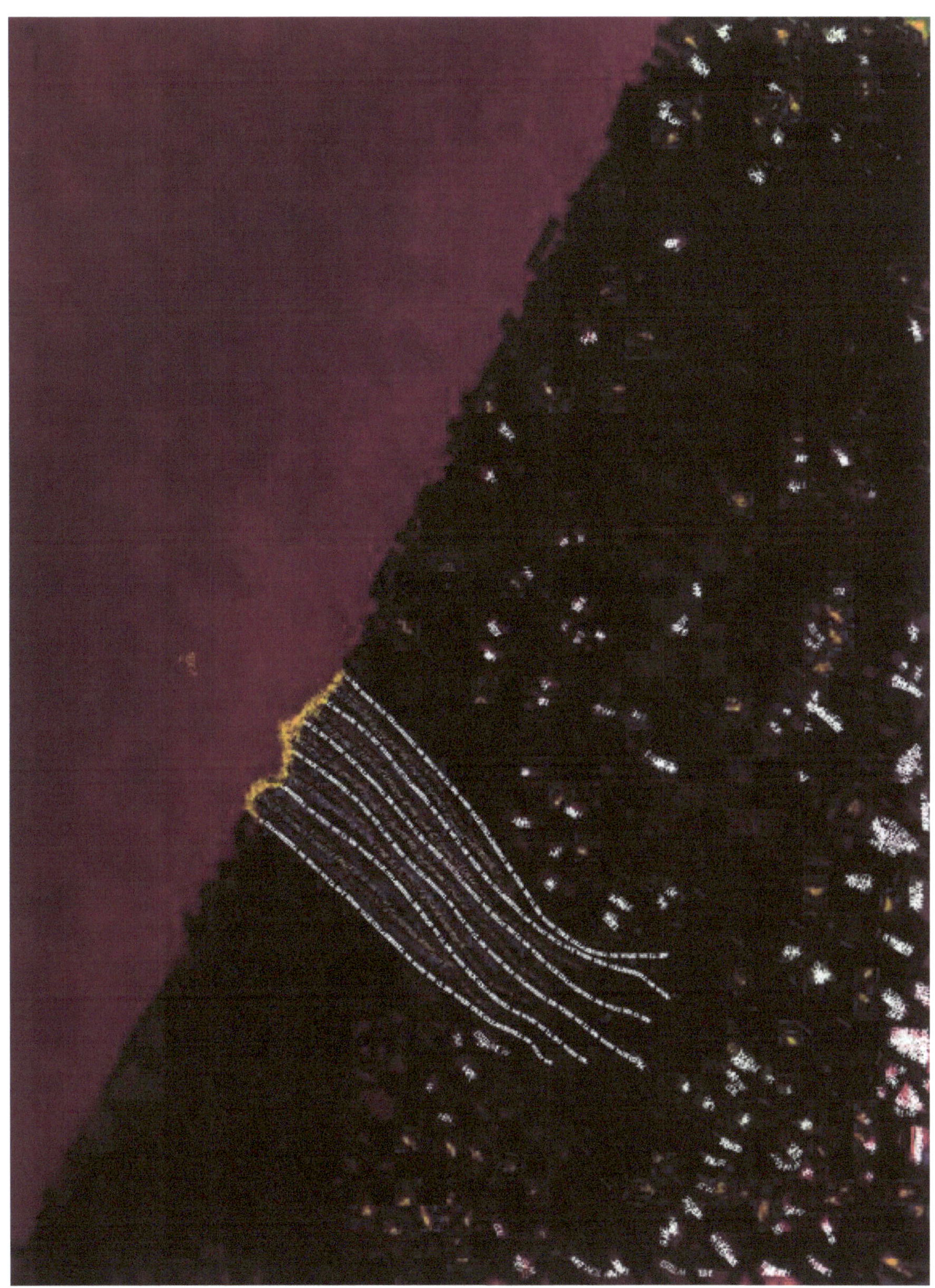

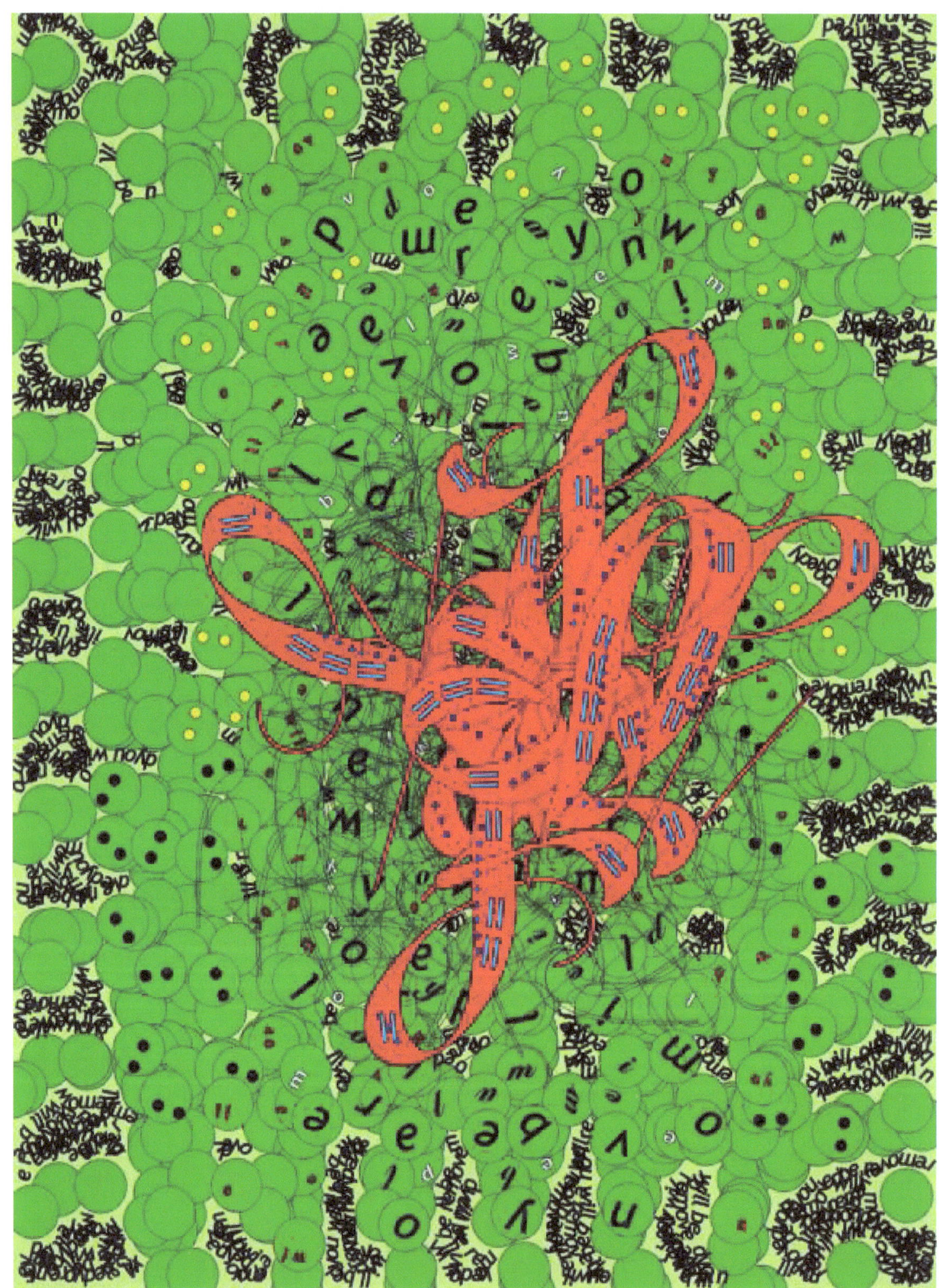

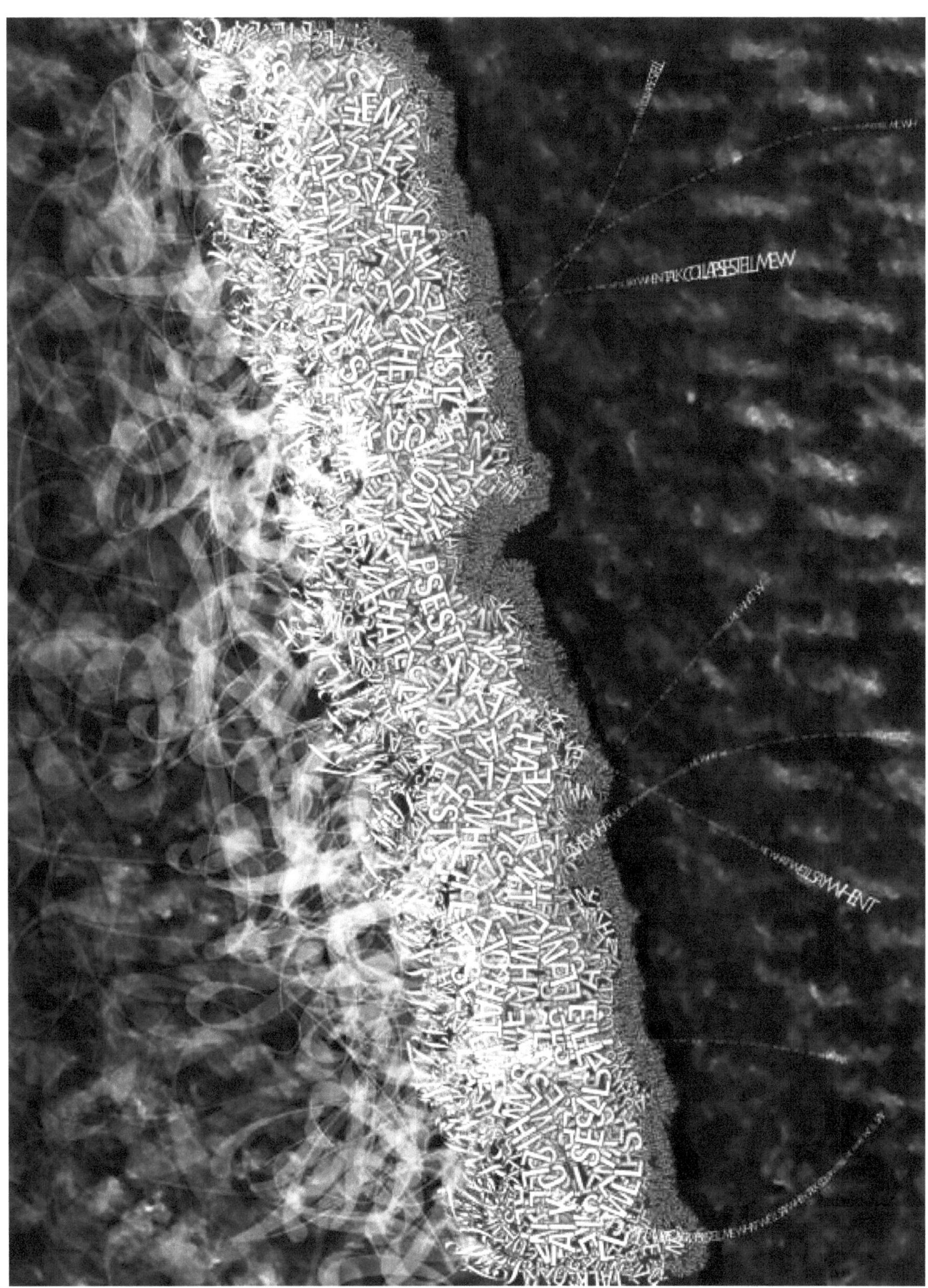

LETTER DENDRITES

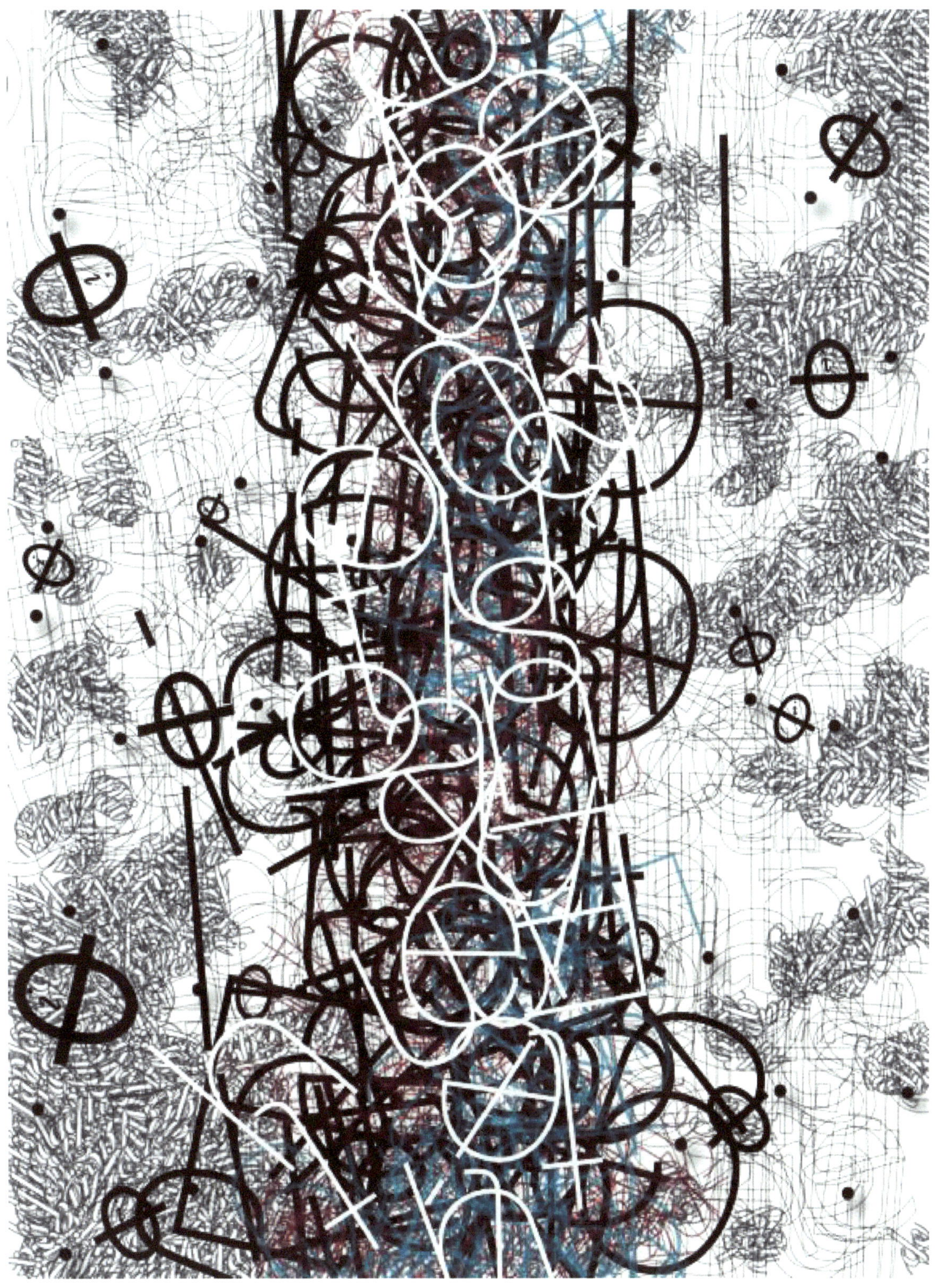

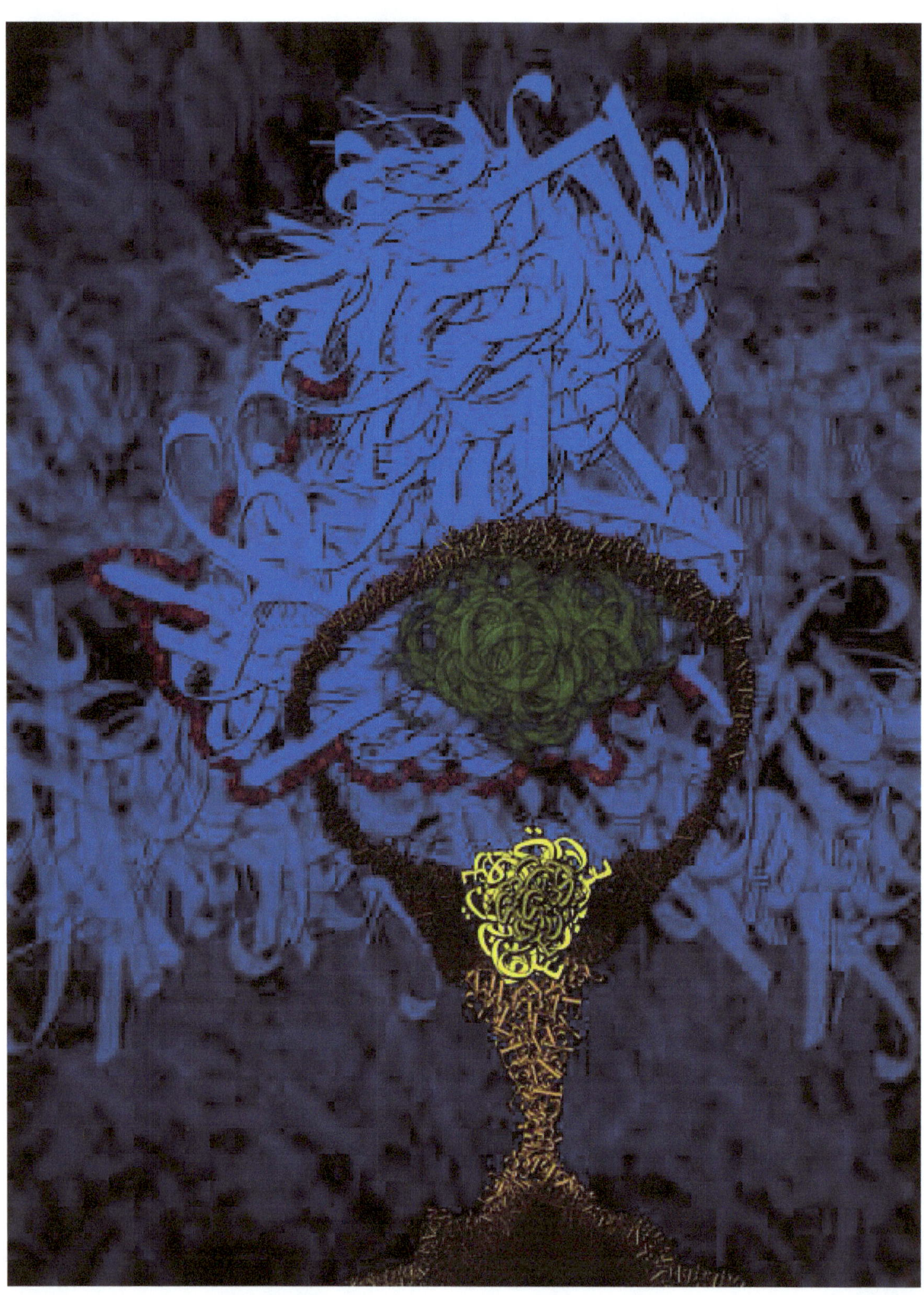

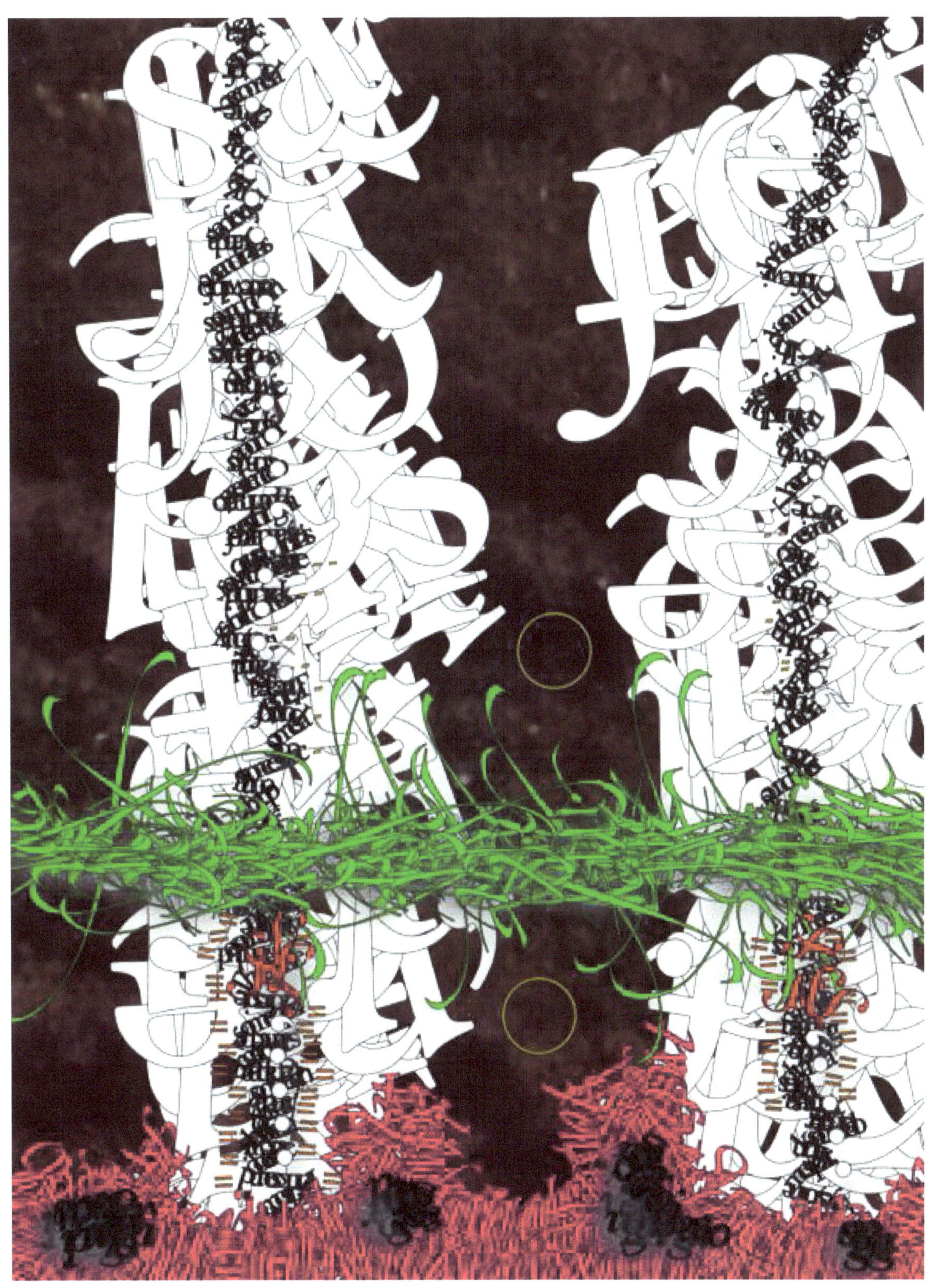

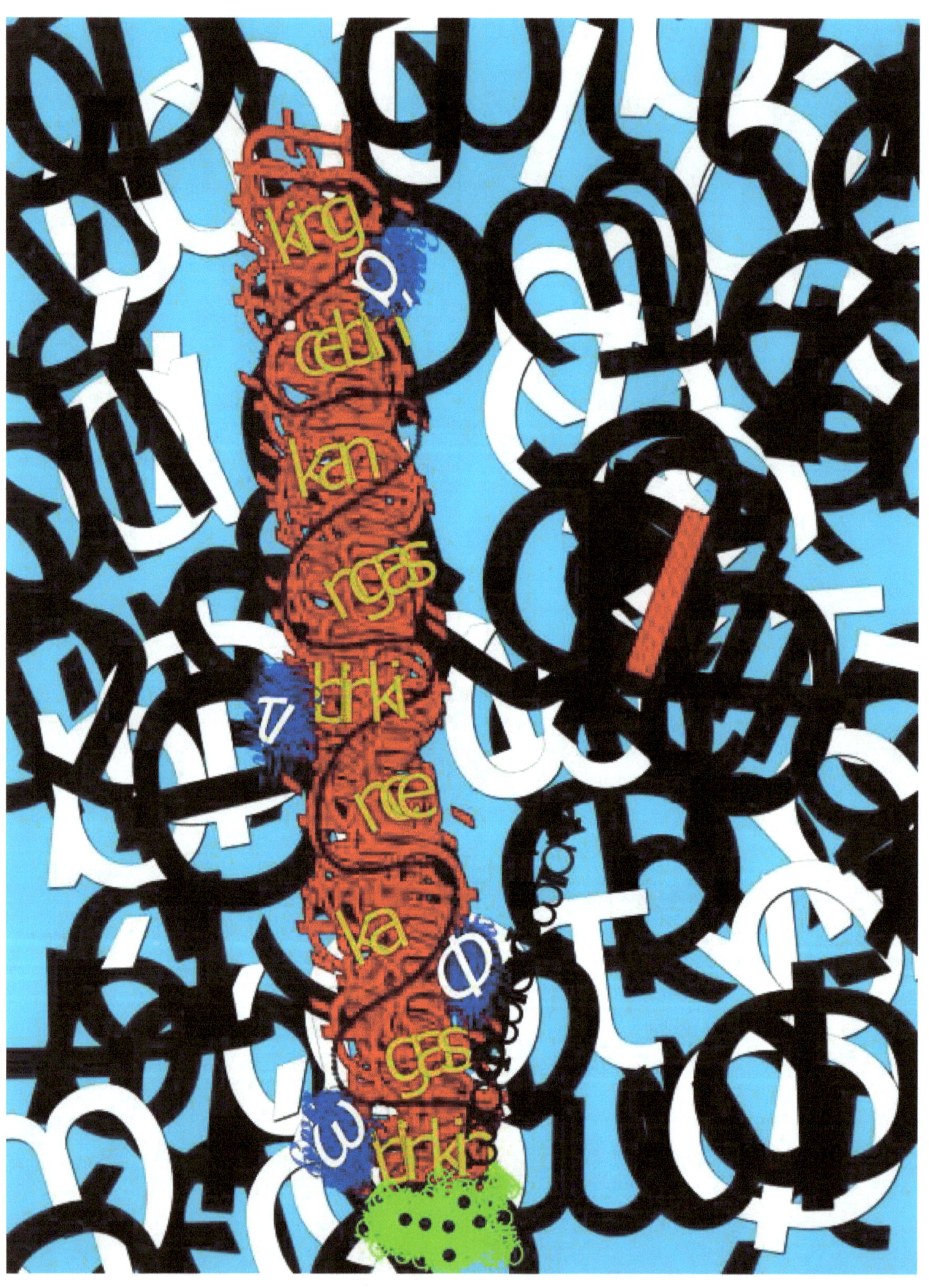

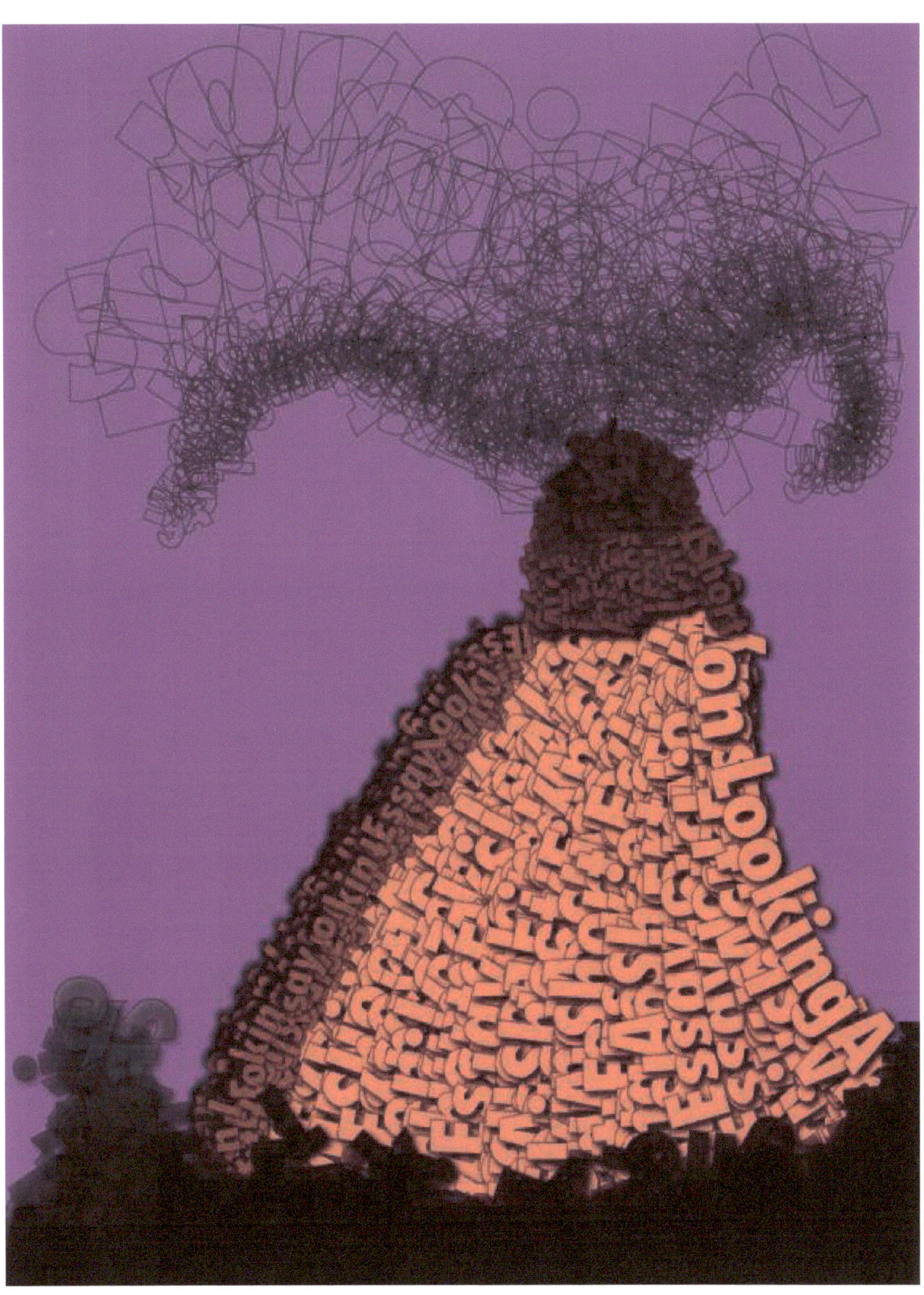
onLookingA

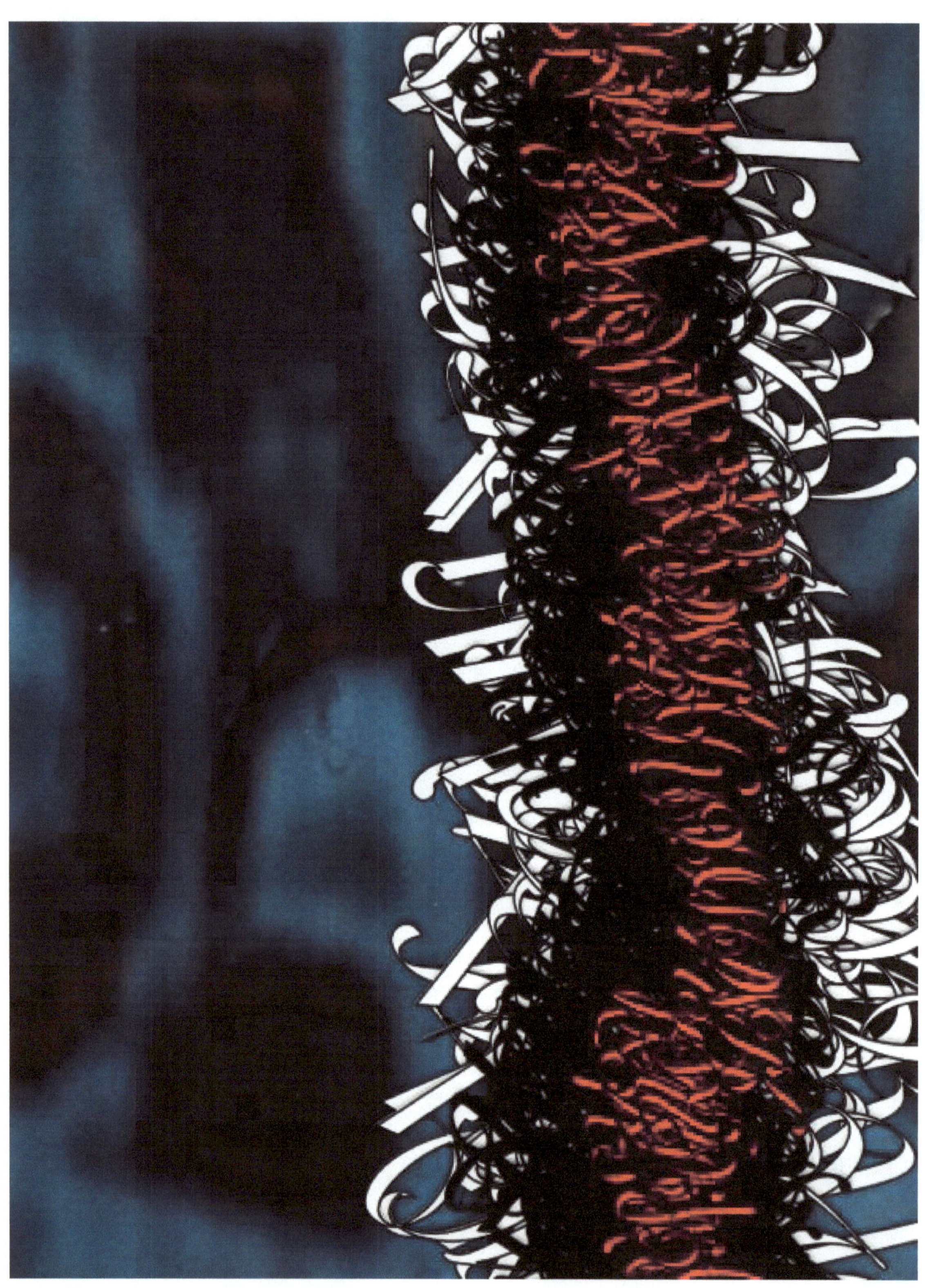

OPINIONS

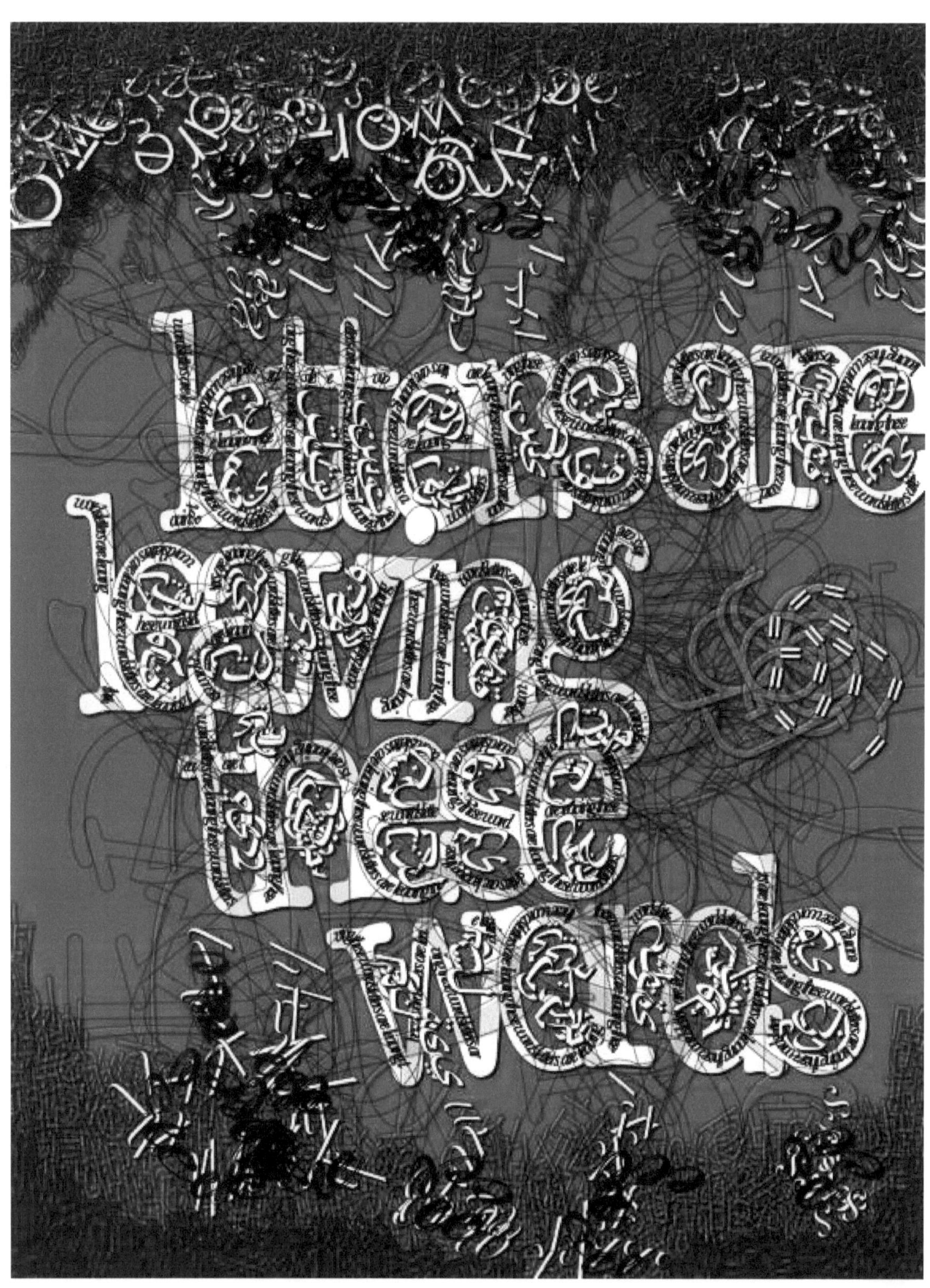
letters are
leaving
these
words

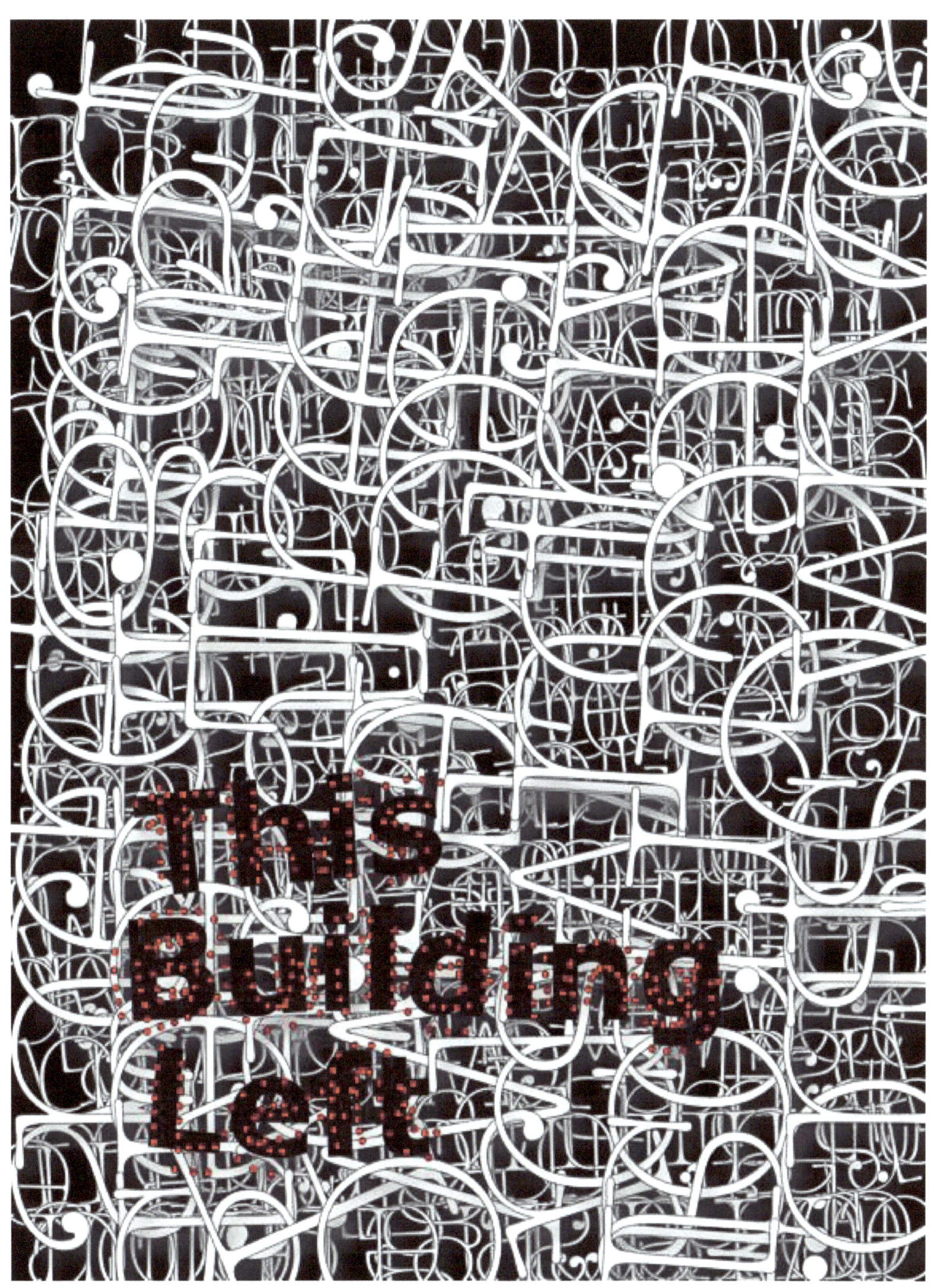
This
Building
Left

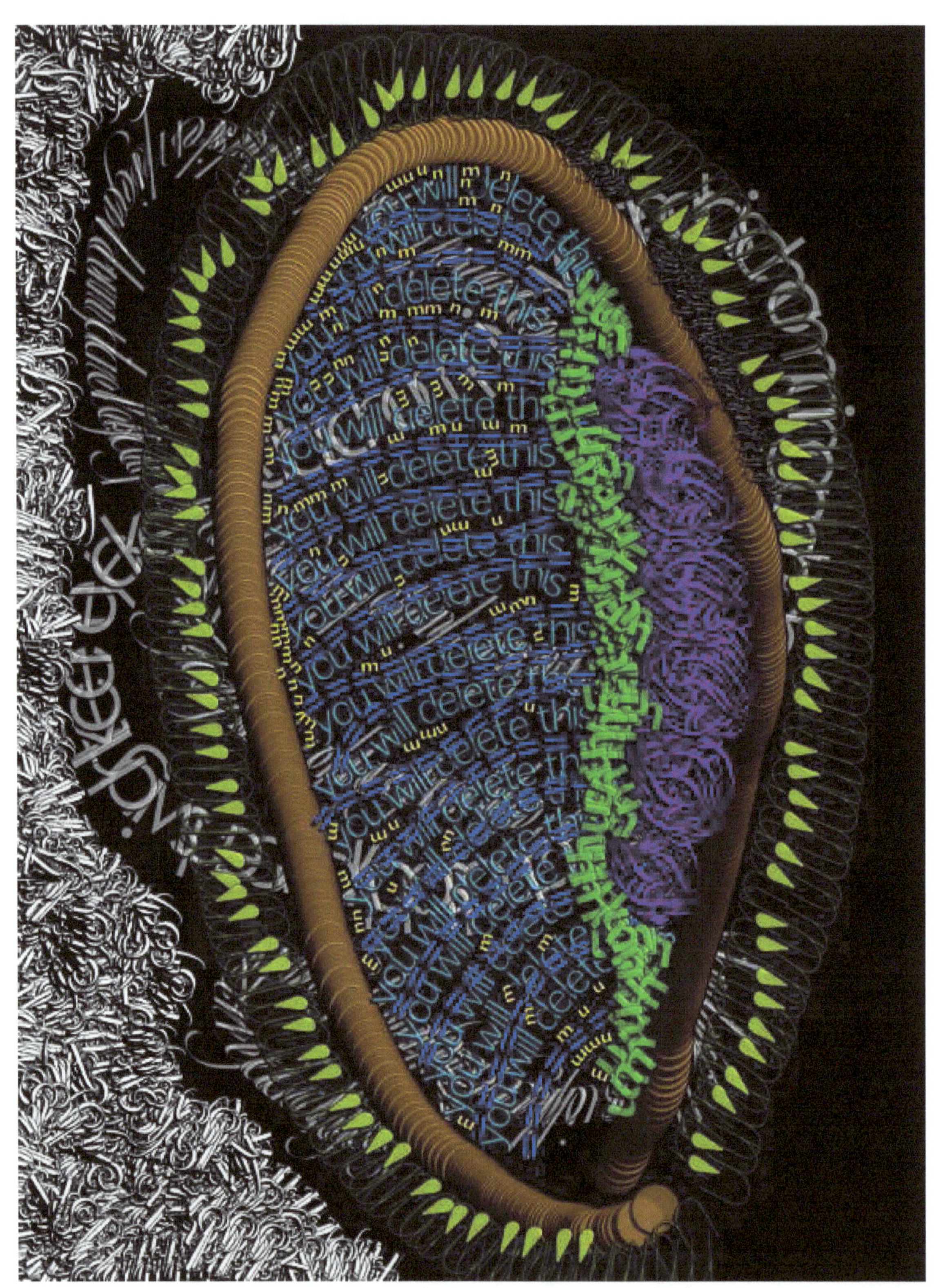
you will delete this

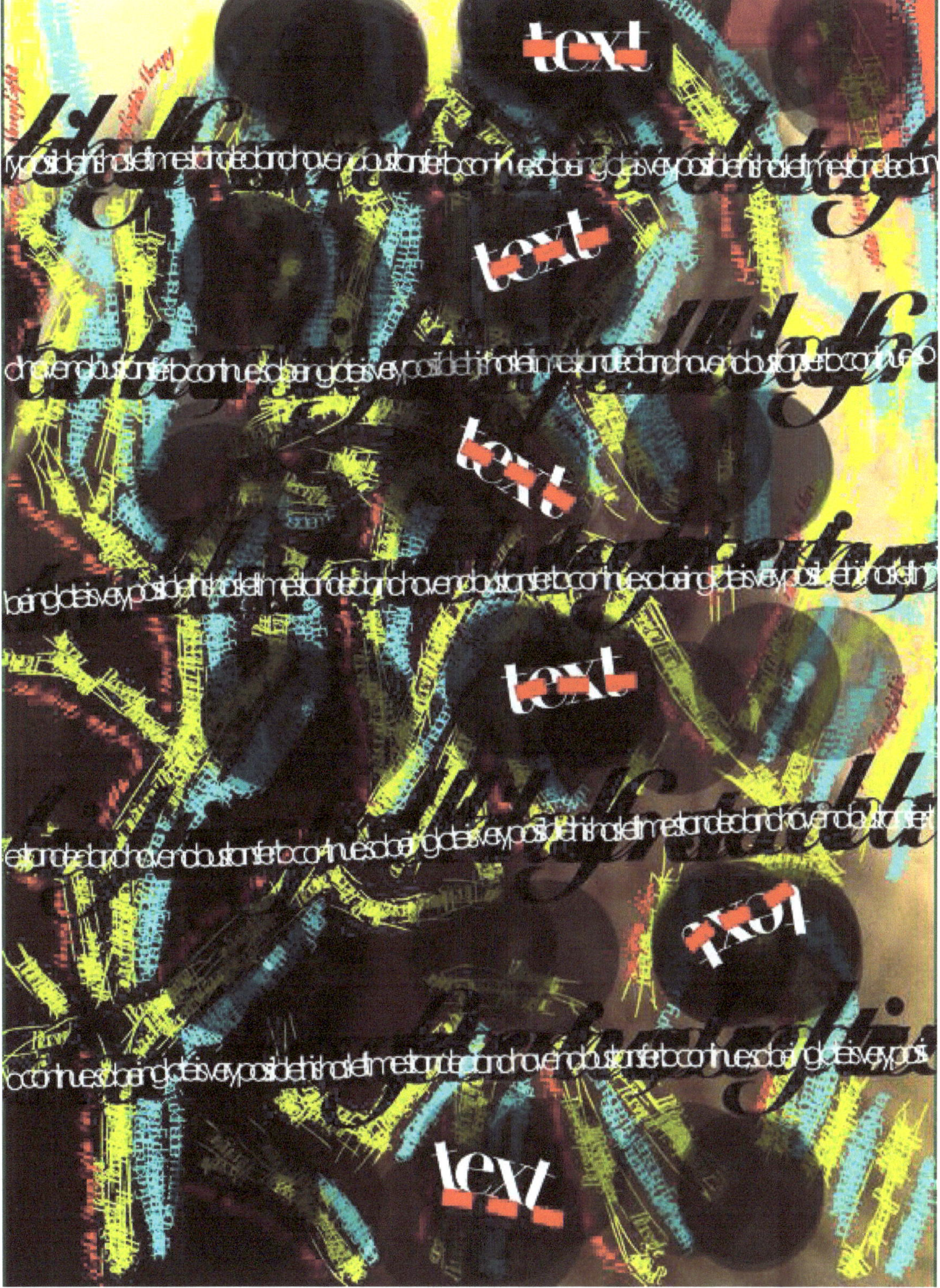
text
text
text
text
text
text

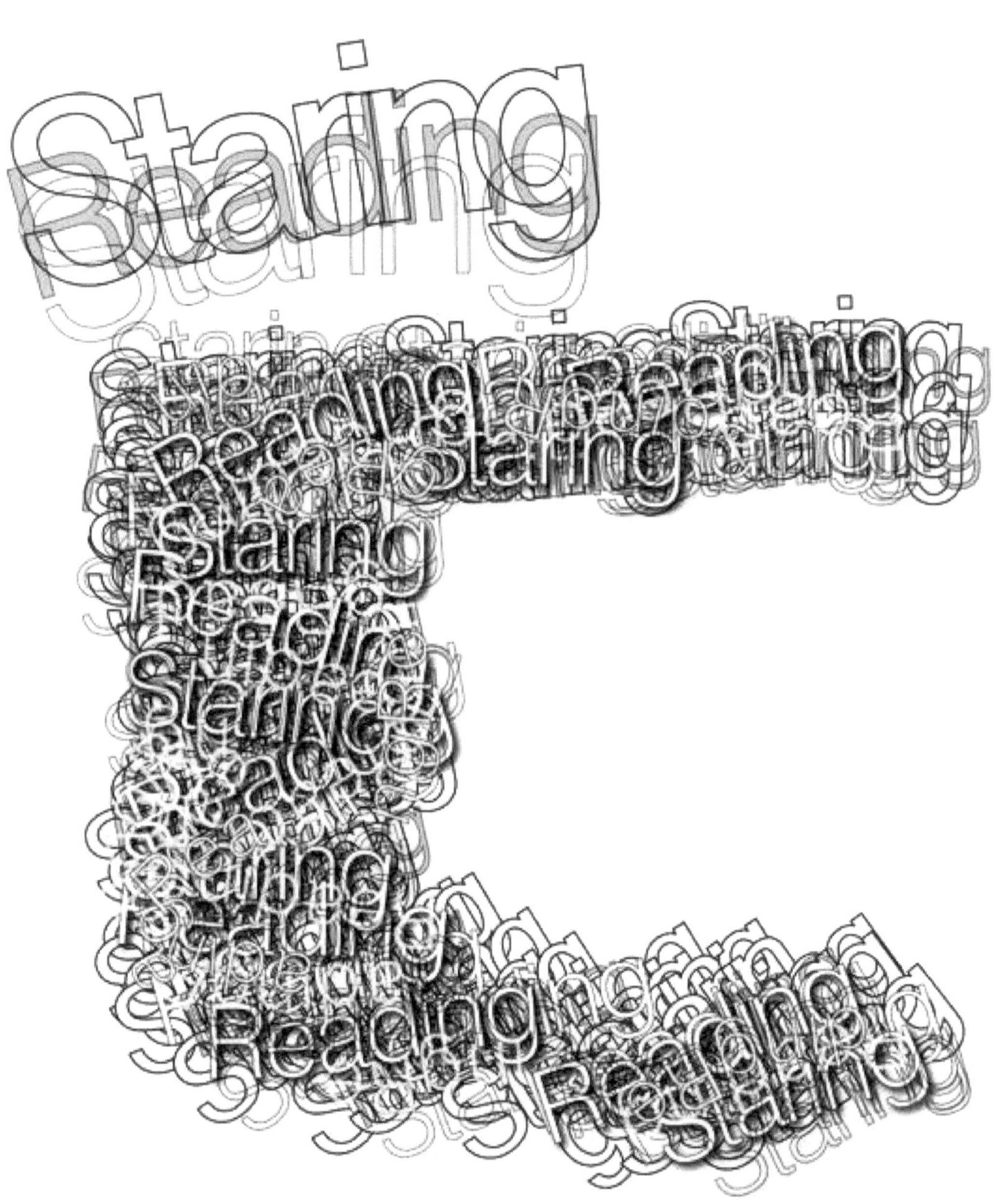

Staring
Staring
Reading
Staring
Reading
Staring
Staring
Reading
Reading
Staring

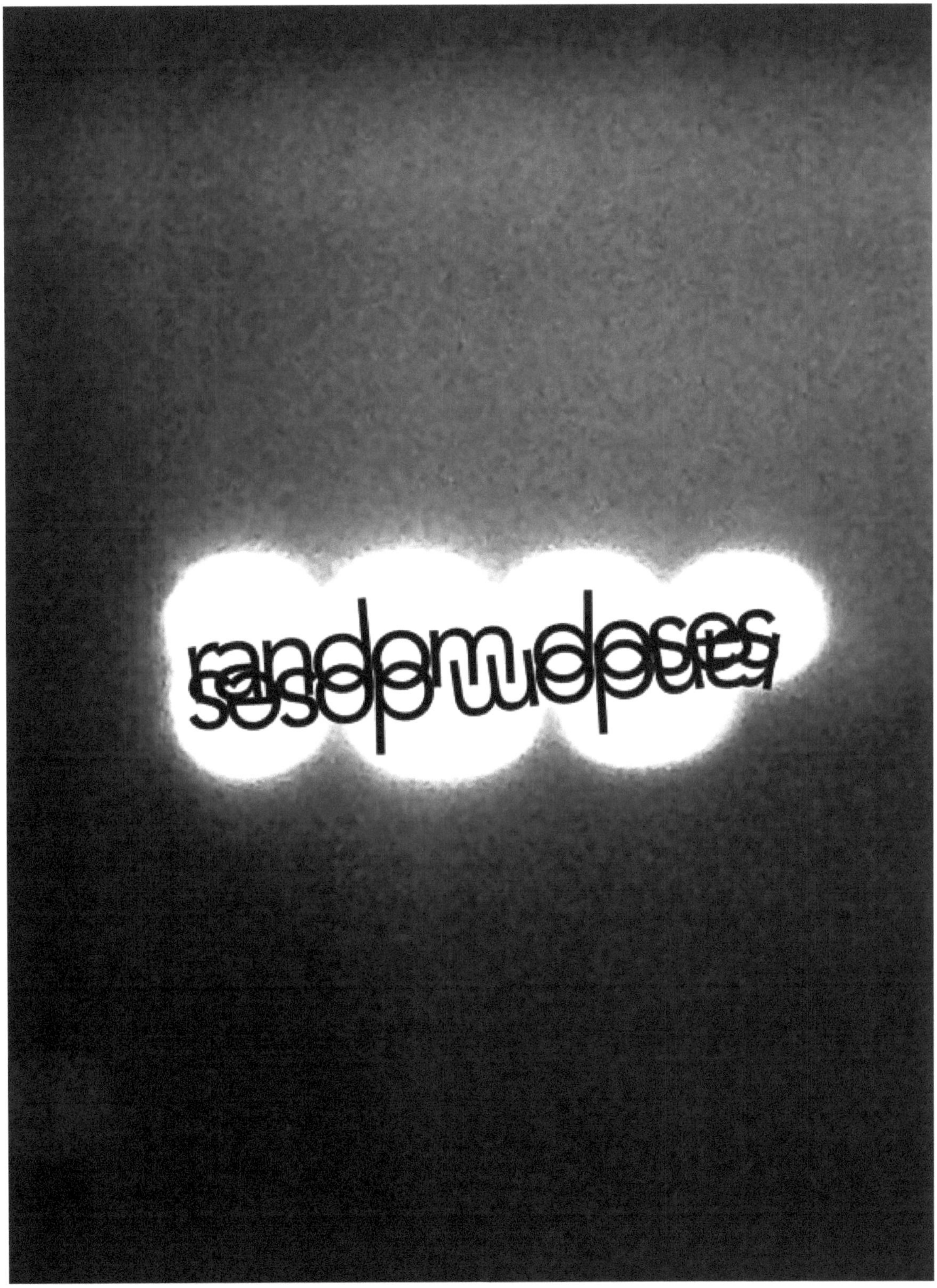

random doses

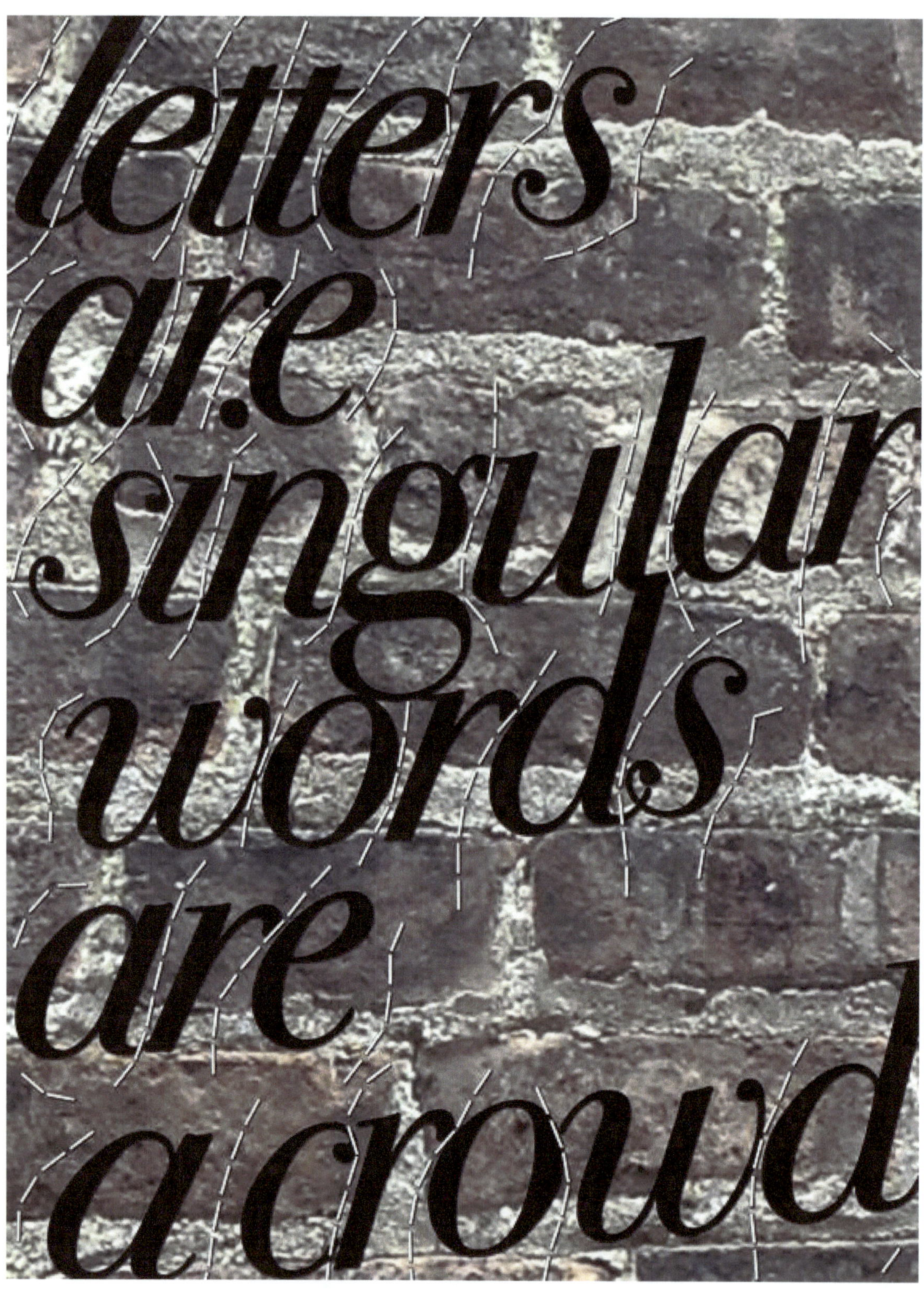

letters
are
singular
words
are
a crowd

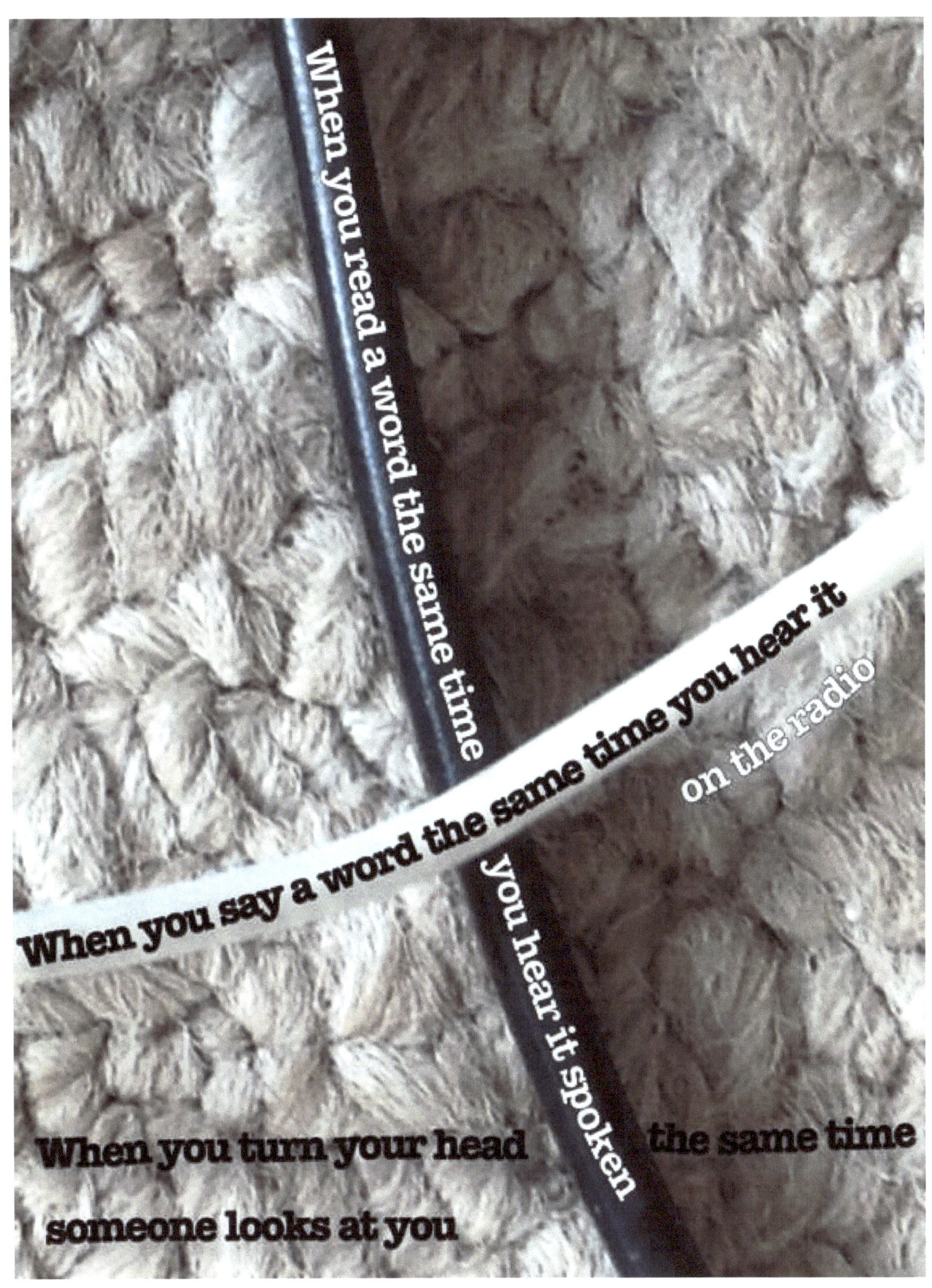

When you read a word the same time
When you say a word the same time you hear it
on the radio
you hear it spoken
When you turn your head
the same time
someone looks at you

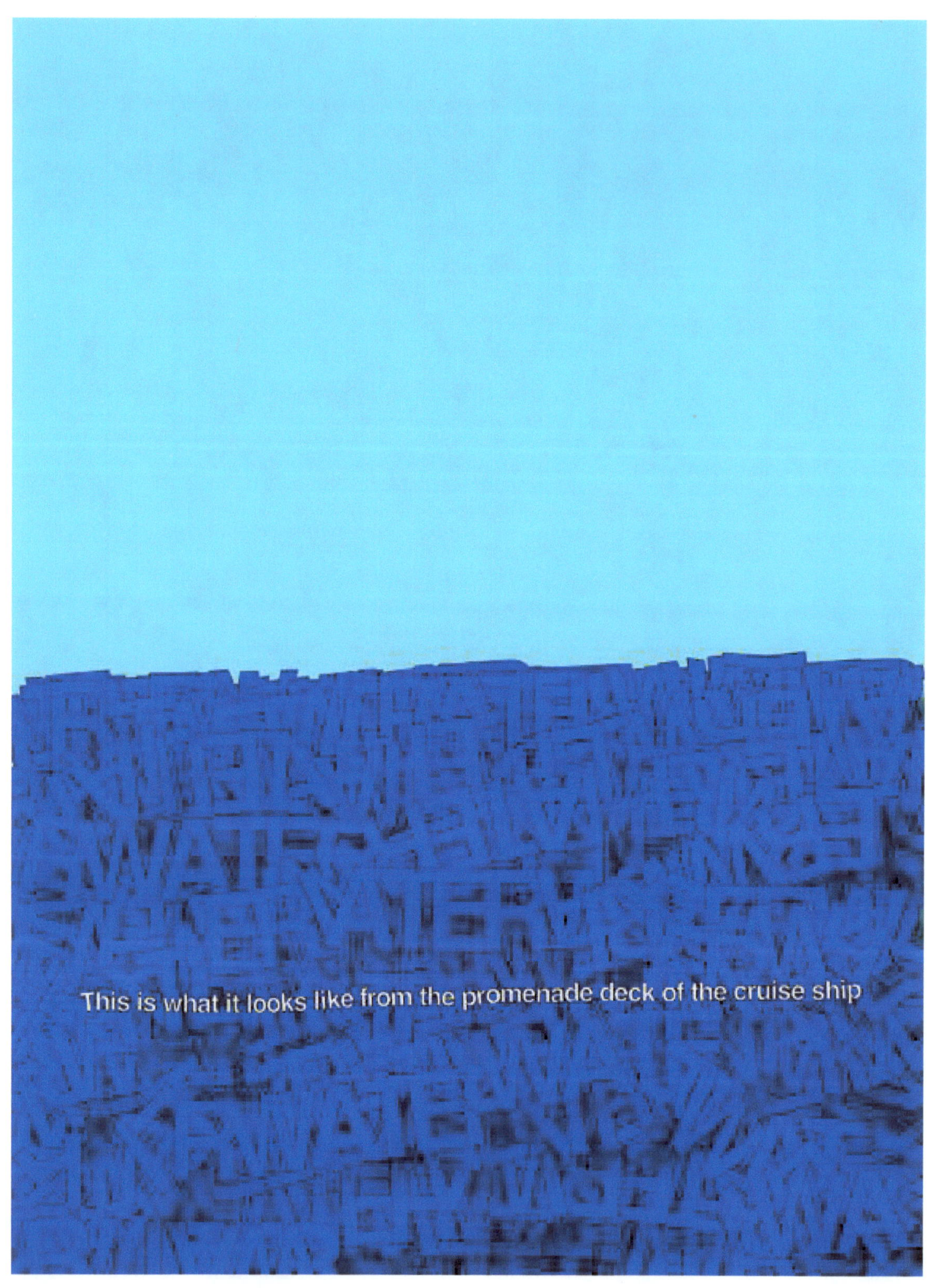

This is what it looks like from the promenade deck of the cruise ship

MISCELLANEOUS COMPOSITIONS

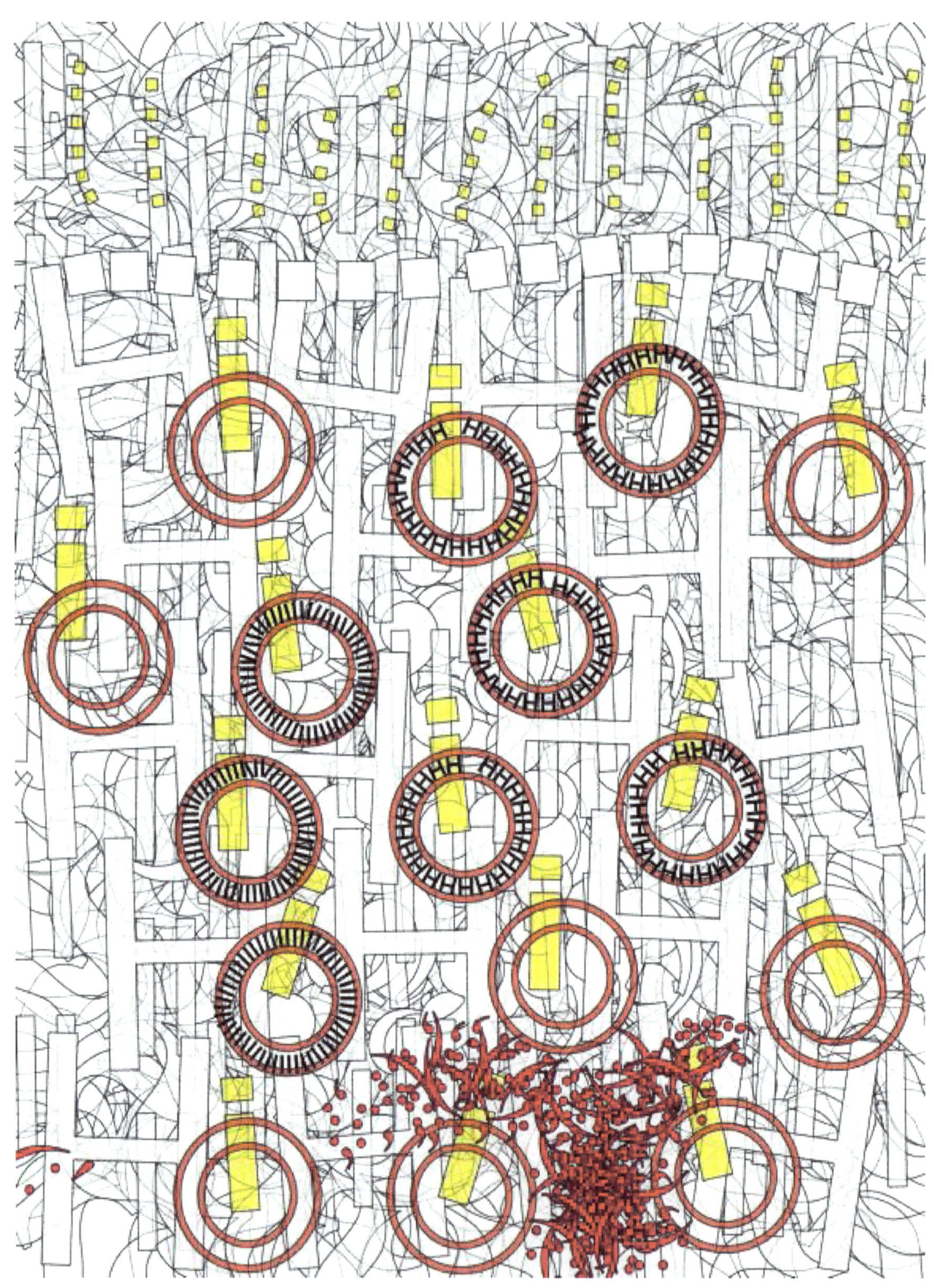

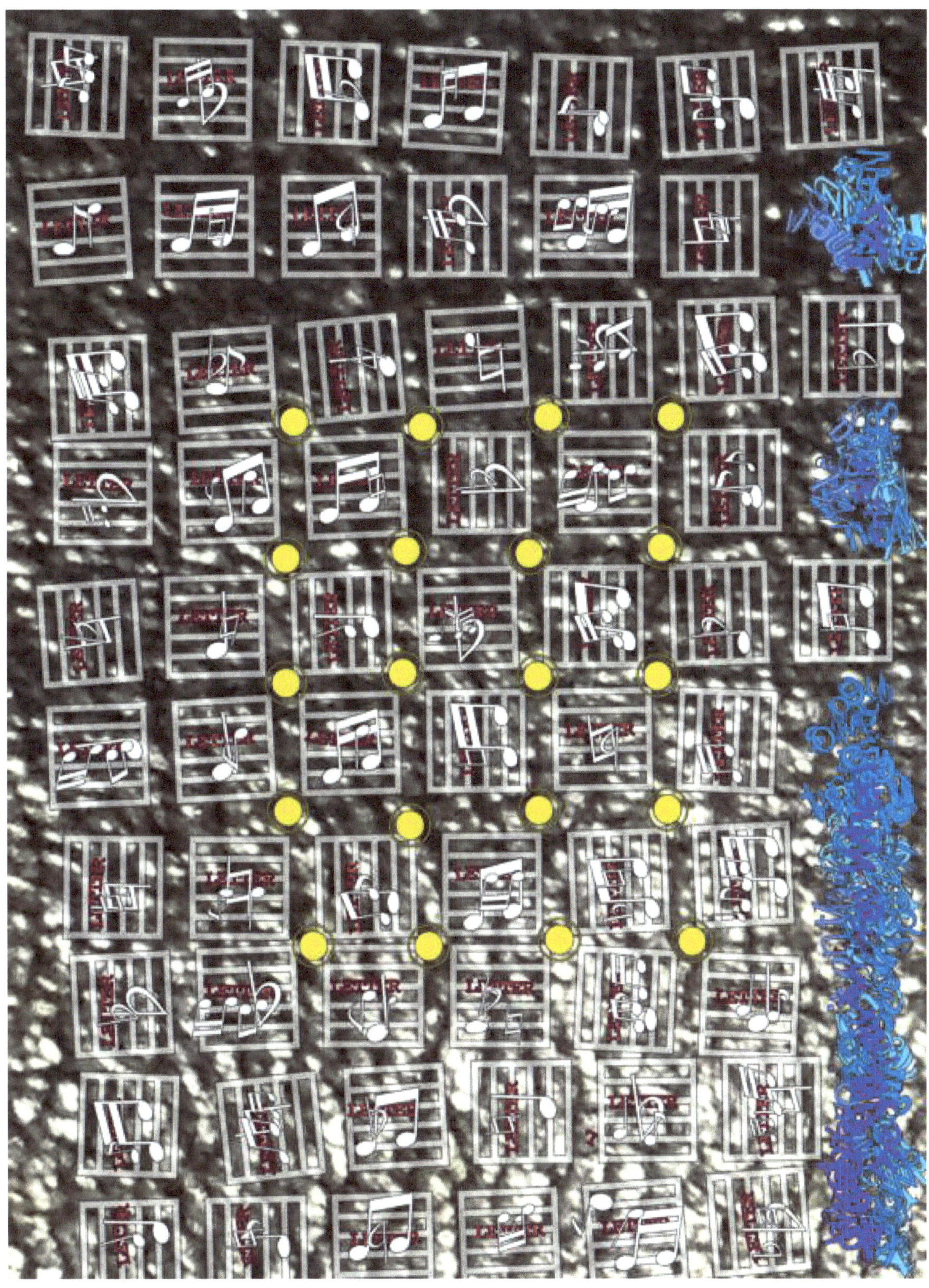

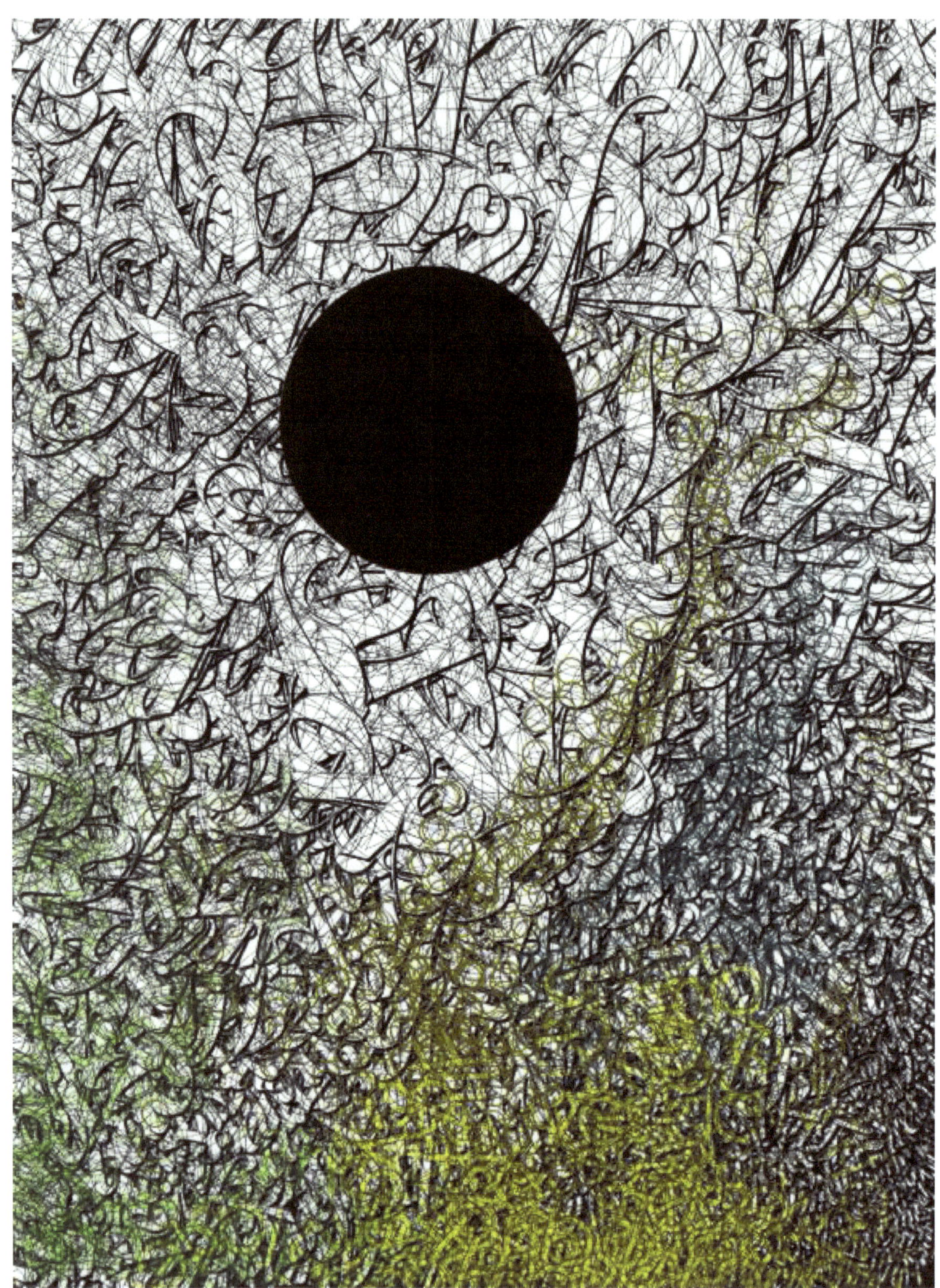

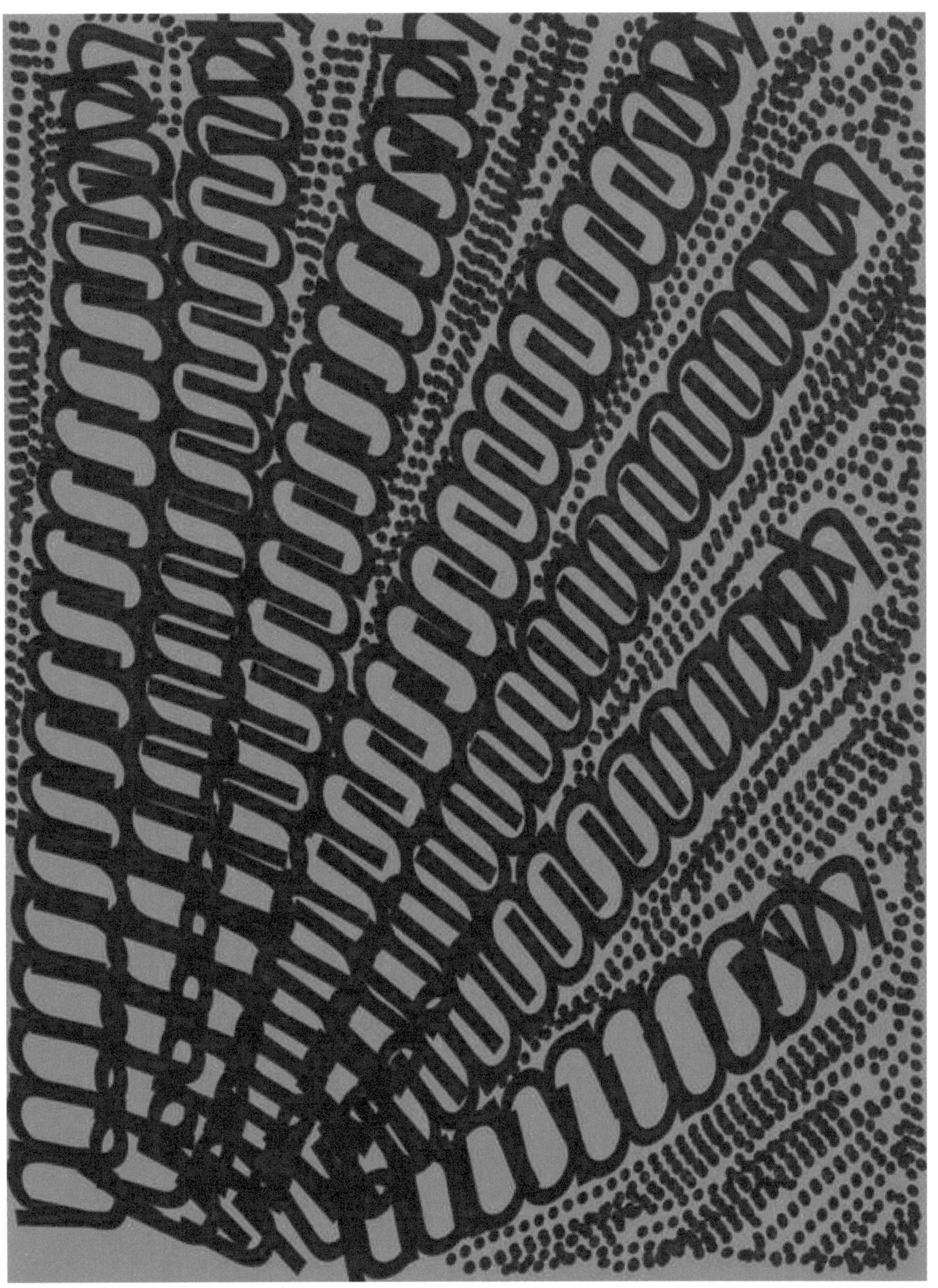

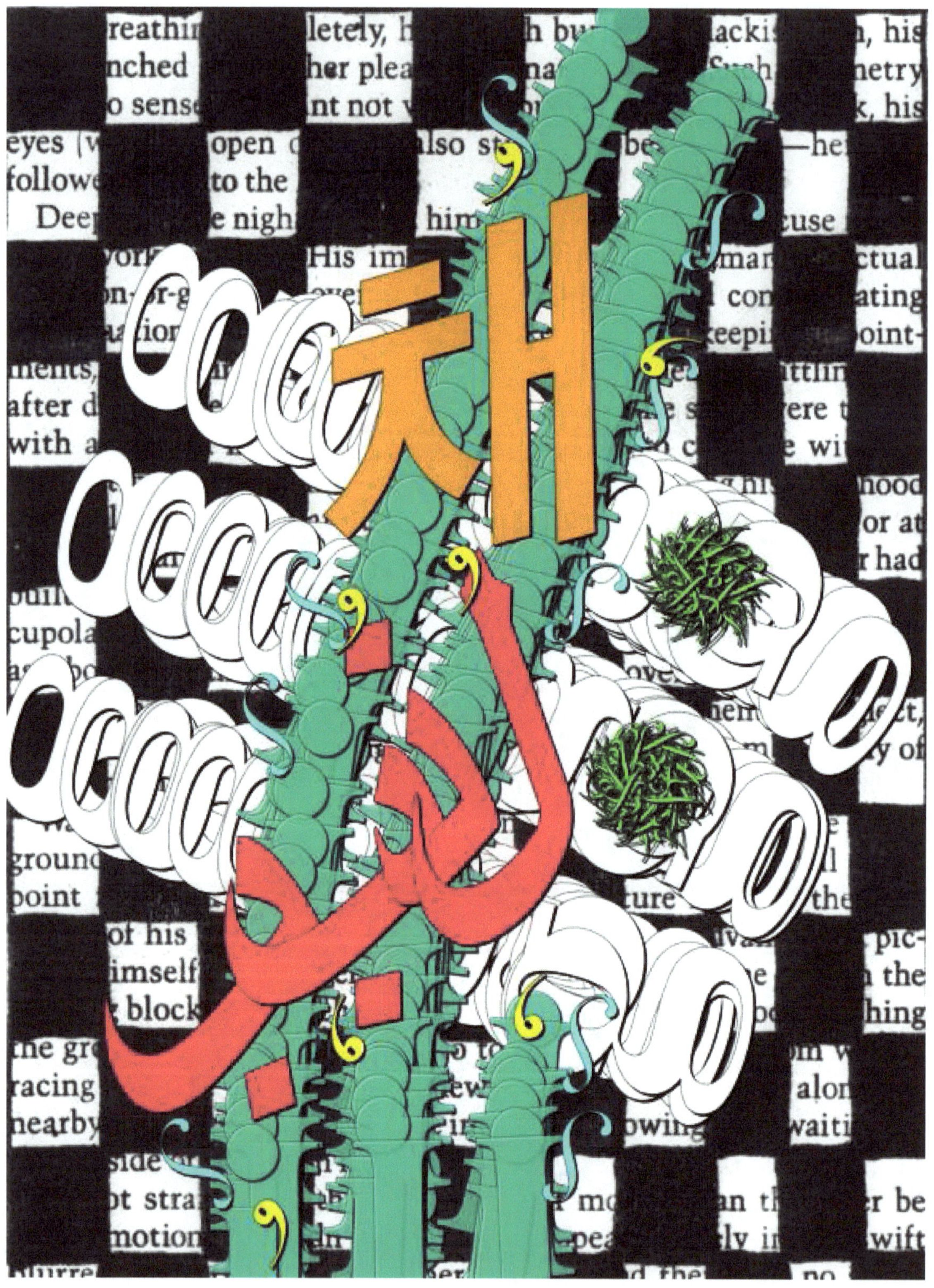

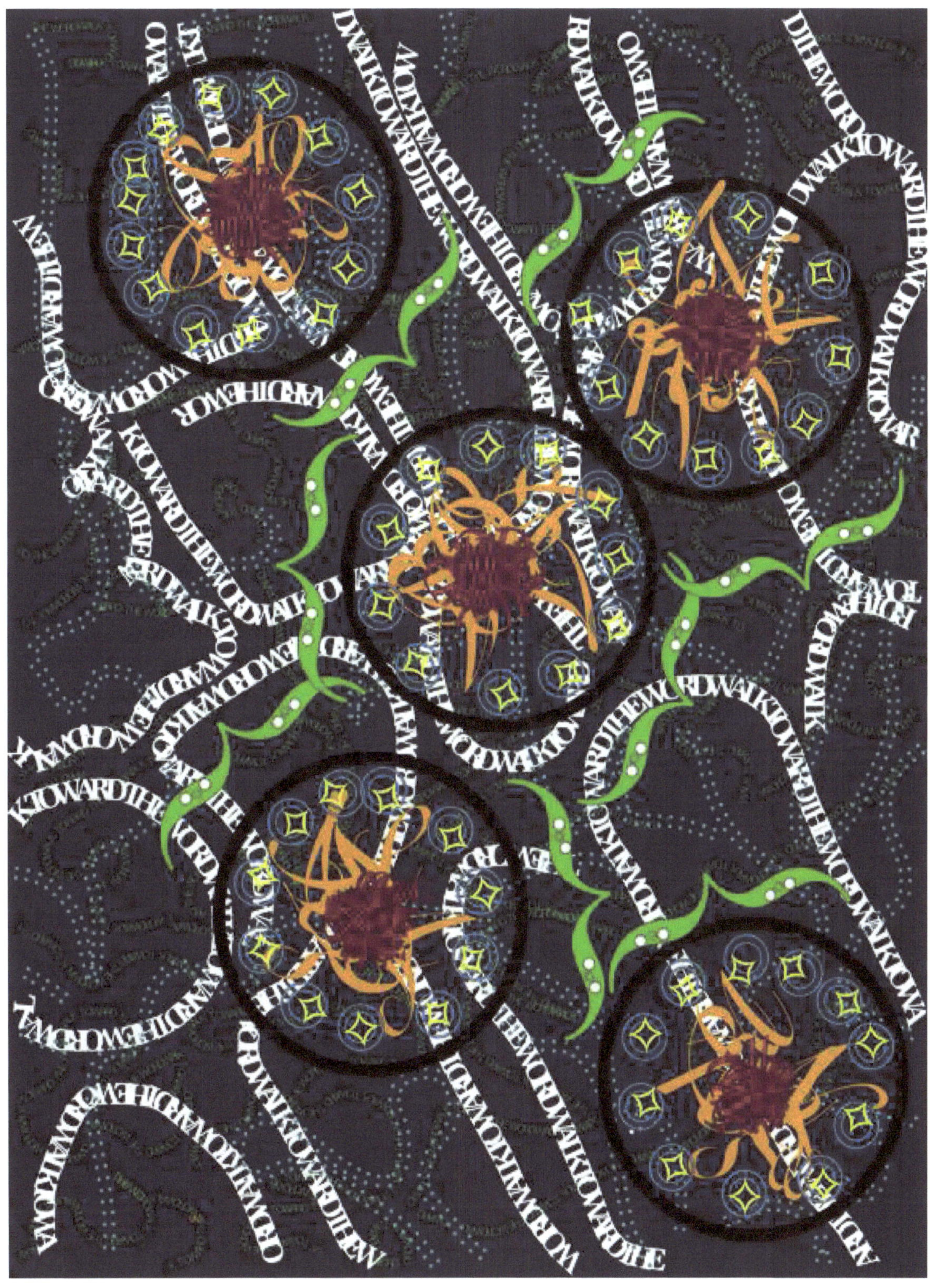